Praise for *Direct Your Own Life*

"Efren and Chris attack everything they do with a spirit and a level of enthusiasm that we all aspire to have in our work and our lives."
—Ted Sarandos, Chief Content Officer, Netflix

"Confronting your movie on the big screen of life can be daunting...but Efren and Chris have created this masterful guide to get you that standing ovation."
—Rodney Charters, ASC, CSC, Cinematographer, *24*

"There's more good advice in here than in a dozen books from the so-called 'experts.' At the rate these two are going, they'll be running Hollywood in no time."
—Patrick Creadon, award-winning documentary filmmaker, *Wordplay* and *I.O.U.S.A.*

"The secret to success is hidden in these pages!"
—Chantal Claret, Lead Singer, Morningwood

"An entertaining guide for any film-lover who wants to produce a better life for him- or herself!"
—Gill Holland, The Group Entertainment, Producer

"*Direct Your Own Life* will encourage young entrepreneurs not to wait in line for someone else to call their number."
—Pascal Maeder, Founder, Atopia

"The messages in this book are brilliant; I couldn't have put them better myself...so I didn't. This book is essential to anyone with a dream lodged somewhere in the back of his or her mind. Use it and live it!"
—Brian Ach, Celebrity Photographer

HOW TO BE A STAR IN ANY
FIELD YOU CHOOSE!

EFREN RAMIREZ
CHRIS BARRETT

PUBLISHING

New York

© 2008 by Efren Ramirez and Christopher Barrett

Photographs by Jessica Hasselbusch

Published by Kaplan Publishing, a division of Kaplan, Inc.
1 Liberty Plaza, 24th Floor
New York, NY 10006

Printed in the United States of America

June 2008
10 9 8 7 6 5 4 3 2 1

ISBN-13: 978-1-4277-9766-7

Kaplan Publishing books are available at special quantity discounts to use for sales promotions, employee premiums, or educational purposes. Please email our Special Sales Department to order or for more information at *kaplanpublishing@kaplan.com*, or write to Kaplan Publishing, 1 Liberty Plaza, 24th Floor, New York, NY 10006.

For you, the reader

Contents

Introduction

J ust a few years ago, we were learning the ropes at the Sundance Film Festival in Park City, Utah. Chris, a young entrepreneur, was featured in the Canadian documentary *The Corporation* as the world's first corporate-sponsored college student, and he traveled from the East Coast to see his film premiere to an American audience. Efren, a young actor who had long been struggling for his big break, traveled from the West Coast to show off his starring role in the "small" indie film, *Napoleon Dynamite*. At the festival, we each had remarkable experiences. *The Corporation* won high acclaim and the World Cinema Documentary Award, and *Napoleon Dynamite* won a standing ovation and a distribution deal that would launch the film into the hearts of millions of adoring fans across the country.

We both seemed to have won the lottery with the successes of our films at Sundance. Chris was an entrepreneurial college kid, and his partnership with First USA to teach financial responsibility to young people prompted

The Corporation's producers to feature him in their film. Efren had been practicing the art of performing for years, yet he had earned only small, sporadic roles until he turned down a part in a movie with a $100 million budget for the lead in an independent film. By opening ourselves up to every humble opportunity, we struck a gold mine of opportunities when our projects blew up at one of the biggest film festivals in the world. But our success wasn't happenstance; as you will see through the pages of this book, we had been moving toward these achievements for years; we had been directing our own lives.

The two of us met at that 2004 Sundance Film Festival while having a blast at all of the parties, screenings, and events. Though we were very different people from completely different backgrounds, we had a lot in common: We were each enjoying the fruits of our hard work and our willingness to be a part of something special.

One of the most important things we have done with our experience was to share our secrets for success with students on high school and college campuses across the country. By talking with these students, it became clear to us that many young people have no faith in their ability to achieve their dreams. Whether they have been discouraged by their families, dissuaded by their friends, or disillusioned by their teachers, most people think that being able to direct their own lives is just a fantasy. Many believe that real life means working 9 to 5. As we listened to these students, we discovered some key points about achieving dreams that anyone can learn and integrate into his or her life. As these principles became clearer, we decided to share them with others through this book.

We want you, our reader, to learn that life isn't lived within the confines of a career; rather, living a successful life means embracing the limitless world of opportunities and allowing yourself to explore any endeavor.

This is what it means to direct your own life: Dream big, work hard, and be open to opportunities. Don't wait for someone to present an opportunity to you—be the director, screenwriter, and producer of your own choices, decisions, and direction.

Directing your own life is not just a fantasy. You *can* make a life out of your dreams. If you are unsure what you want to do with your life or you don't know how to accomplish your dream, *Direct Your Own Life* is for you.

Direct Your Own Life is a collection of battle stories, advice, and hands-on steps you can take to overcome your fears of failure, find direction, and accomplish your dreams. We've shared stories from our own lives and experience and presented some stories from other young people who are living their dreams.

In the pages of *Direct Your Own Life,* you'll discover that living a successful life means embracing the limitless world of opportunities and allowing yourself to dream. The only way you can give back to the world is to make yourself happy first. We can't wait to see what dreams you come up with—and to see you achieve those dreams. If two regular guys like us can do it, you can, too.

ACT I

PRE-PRODUCTION:
CREATE YOUR LIFE SCRIPT

CHAPTER 1

Develop Your Life Script

Every movie starts with a script. But how does a script get written? Well, you need Final Draft (a screenwriting program), a Word document, or a piece of paper. But much more importantly, you need an idea.

Where does the idea come from? From brainstorming, talking, questioning, and staying open to life and all it has to offer. Some scripts are inspired by a person, real or imagined; others by events or phenomena that happen in real life. Every script contains description, stage directions, and dialogue, which amount to a plan that the cast and crew share to make a film.

We all have a story to tell. You are the screenwriter of your own life. So at this point in your life, when you are "figuring it out," it's absolutely necessary that you brainstorm ideas about what you want your life and work to be about. When you discover the idea for your life—what your dream is—you literally uncover your life's purpose.

CHRIS: One morning while relaxing at the hotel before our next college tour, we saw Tiger Woods give a press conference on TV. He was wearing his Nike logo hat and talking about his latest golf tour. Luke and I looked at each other and said, "That's it!"

You're always surrounded by inspiration, but do you know it when you see it? For example, how many times have you watched an airplane as it crosses the sky? Have you ever imagined becoming an airline pilot, a flight attendant, or a travel agent? Inspiration is all around you, if you know where to look. To find it, you must go out and experience life with your eyes wide open.

If you don't know how to find inspiration, your first step is to start looking for it. Because we do that all the time, we're going to help you find the ideas to use in your life script. Whatever you want to do, there's absolutely no reason why you can't do it—and a lot of reasons why you can.

Look for Raw Material

An idea for your life script might be right in front of you. Ask yourself, "What do I enjoy?" Let's say you enjoy doodling in your spare time. How would you feel about making drawing more than just a hobby? Or maybe you enjoy playing video games and telling other people how to beat Slash's avatar in Guitar Hero III. Think about how gratifying it would be to turn all of those hours you spend in front of your Nintendo

Wii into a career. Perhaps you like camping and the outdoors. Discovery might be the most important part of your life. Try to identify your passions. Make a list!

Once you have identified a few of your passions, go deeper. For example, if you love food, do you want to become a chef? A restaurant critic? An exporter/importer of foods from around the world? A cookbook writer? An inventor of kitchen appliances? The possibilities surrounding each idea are literally unlimited, even though they all start from the same place.

> EFREN: The first time I tried acting in high school, I knew that I had found something that helped me express myself, and a dream was born.

Naming what you enjoy doing is the first step toward living the life that you want. Remember waking up as a kid and looking forward to a special day, such as the last day of school, Christmas morning, or the first day of a vacation? By identifying and choosing to do what you love, every day suddenly becomes that special day, because every day you'll get to do exactly what you want. This feeling—and not money—is the most fulfilling reward you'll ever receive for hard work.

Getting paid to do what you want is nice, and everyone needs to make a living. But what's more important than money is doing what makes you happy. Chances are, the happier you are while you're working, the more and better work you'll do. And most times, that translates into being paid more. The goal here is to focus on making yourself happy; rewards will come the more you believe in your work, as Efren learned when he turned down a studio picture for a lead role in an unknown, independent, low-budget project called *Napoleon Dynamite*.

 DIRECTOR'S NOTES: If the idea of getting paid to do something you enjoy sounds like your dream job, congratulations! You just discovered your purpose in life.

Take Inspiration from Others

Before a screenwriter even starts thinking about writing a movie, he asks himself this crucial question: "What's my screenplay about?" Sometimes that's not such an easy question to answer. Often, writers look for inspiration in other movies they've seen. Then they decide how their movie idea is both similar to and different from already existing movies.

You can apply this same principle in your own life. Start by looking at other people's stories. Begin with the people around you—people you know personally, strangers you happen to see during the day, or people you see on television or read about in magazines and newspapers. Really look at them. How do they make a living? How do they spend their days? What is important to them? Which parts of their lives do you admire? Which would you like to have for yourself? Which parts of their lives do you dislike and want to avoid?

Here's a tip: as you evaluate other people's lives, instead of focusing on what they have, focus on what they do. Let's say you admire a famous movie star. For fun, let's say you admire Angelina Jolie. There are many who would want her fame, her power, her lifestyle, even her family. But Angelina could not have succeeded as a movie star without first dedicating her life to acting. If you think you might want to be an actor, you have to consider how it would feel to devote your life to acting, not how it would feel to have money and fame.

Of course, being a famous actor certainly will make you a lot of money, but to become good enough to command $8 million a picture, you have to put in a lot of time, effort, and hard work. Many will pour more time, effort, and hard work into an endeavor and not see very much money for it. Ask yourself, "Would I love to do this even if I were paid nothing?" If your answer is no, let the idea go. Be honest—you don't love your idea without the fantasy of a big paycheck attached to it. And if you don't love your dream independently of how much it could pay, your effort will be forced, your work will be poor, and you won't make any money anyway. Leave that life to those who can truly answer yes.

If you are honest with yourself as you observe others' lives, you will find the vocation or lifestyle that you would love no matter what the paycheck is. Remember, you don't want just any dream; you want *the* dream that will make your life the best it can possibly be. Finding out what you don't want to do is important, too, because each time you react negatively to what other people do ("I wouldn't want to travel for my job" or "I don't want to work in an office"), you're one step closer to finding what you do want to do.

The more you find out how others are living their dreams, the more likely you'll find a life that looks like what you want your own life to be. Don't worry if you don't see your own life resembling the lives of others. Our lives don't look exactly like anyone else's: Efren pursues the roles that are right for him, and Chris lives a life that is not defined by a 9-to-5 job. That's what we've chosen.

Remember that if you can't find anyone doing the thing you'd love to do (in this book or in your life), that doesn't mean what you want doesn't exist. It simply means that you need to start looking beyond the world around you. This is where your imagination takes center stage.

☆ **DIRECTOR'S NOTES:** To find inspiration for your dreams, focus on what other people do, not on what they have.

Use Your Imagination

If, after you've observed as many people's lives as you can, you still don't have an idea of what direction your life script should take, tap into your creative side and start making things up.

CHRIS: My friend Luke and I wanted to go to college far from our hometown, but we didn't know how we could afford it. From that problem, we came up with a solution that shaped our lives in amazing ways.

Lots of people are born into a world where they feel their options are limited. Maybe they don't know anyone who is doing something they would want to do, or maybe there seem to be too many barriers to exploring a new idea. But this doesn't mean that they, or you, have to give up on living a satisfying life. The first step toward that life is using your imagination. Expanding your mind and world are essential to achieving success. The journey is all part of the process.

Let's try some brainstorming. Do you want to run your own restaurant? Design you own clothing line? Run the Boston Marathon? Sell an invention? Write a novel or screenplay? Travel around the world? Write and sell a computer program?

Don't worry if your idea sounds far-fetched or impossible. Don't worry if it takes you out of your neighborhood or hometown. Remember, all ideas, like all movies, start in the imagination, and your imagination is unlimited unless *you* impose limits.

Developing your imagination is something you can do for free. It can be as easy as sitting on a park bench and watching strangers pass by. What does that woman with the tiny dog in a designer purse eat for breakfast? Where is that short, bald guy going so quickly? Everyday occurrences can jolt you into a creative reverie, if you just let them. Some will even give you ideas for your life script.

Be Willing to Change

Even if you aren't quite sure what you want to do with your life, one thing is certain: you'll need to change. For more options to become available to you, you might need to do the following:

- Learn new habits (and get rid of old ones).
- Meet new people (and get rid of your shyness).
- Live in new places (and get out of your comfort zone).

Change is inevitable, and the difference between success- ful and not-so-successful people isn't whether they change or not but whether they choose to change or just let change happen to them. Learn to embrace the possibility of change. It isn't always comfortable at first, but in the long run, change can take you to wonderful places. Chris often goes out of his comfort zone to meet new people, and they have often helped him to further develop his life script.

Every time Hollywood makes a new movie, the direc- tor, actors, and film crew have to travel to new locations that they've never seen before. When you start pursuing your dreams, whatever they might be, your life will have to change and take you to new places you've never seen before, too. Don't be scared; be excited. Your life is about to take a major turn toward bigger and better things, and the best part is, you'll be the one in control. In Efren's case, the role in *Napoleon Dynamite* took him from East Los Angeles to Preston, Idaho.

Any dream worth achieving is probably going to take time to reach. But if you truly enjoy what you're doing, does it really matter?

 DIRECTOR'S NOTES: Whatever you want to do, there's no reason why you can't do it.

Develop Your Idea into a Story

In Hollywood, every movie starts out with an idea, but that idea is useless until it's turned into a script. A script is exactly what you need for your own dreams. Every dream gives you a direction, but you need a script, or plan, that shows you how to get there. A good script is like a great ride: it gets you where you're going and shows you a good time along the way.

You don't have to be a Pulitzer Prize–winning author to create the script of your own life. We'll help you. And don't worry—there is no "right" script. Two different people can pursue the same dream but get there using two different paths. For example, we launched a production company together, but one of us started as an entrepreneur and the other started as an actor.

You've already made a list of the things you enjoy doing, identified and researched the lifestyles of people you admire, and stretched those imagination muscles. Now it's time to start writing.

1. Define what you want in as much detail as possible.

Striving for a dream is like aiming at a target. The more specific your dream, the sharper your aim can be and the more likely you'll hit the target. It's easier to hit the bull's-eye if you see it clearly, but how can you hit the bull's-eye if you don't even know what target you're shooting at?

Let's talk about how to focus your goals. Suppose you love sports. Which sport do you love the most? If you love baseball, get even more specific and ask yourself what you love most about baseball. Is it watching the game? Following your favorite players? Reading about baseball history? Playing shortstop? You could take a hundred different baseball fanatics from all around the world and find a hundred different reasons why they each love baseball.

> EFREN: When I have to memorize a script, I tape notes alongside it, breaking down the character and every detail of the script into its simplest form, so I know I really understand it.

Get as detailed as possible to figure out why you love what you do. If you tell people you want to become a doctor, mention what type of doctor you'd like to be. There's a big difference between being a general practitioner and an open heart surgeon—different day-to-day routines, different specialties, different problems.

Once you've nailed down some of the specifics of your dream, share it with others. In doing this, you'll gain more confidence that you can actually achieve it, and you'll also get a chance to hear how it sounds "out in the world." Do you feel ridiculous or powerful? Don't be surprised if you feel vulnerable when you share your dream with others. You will learn a lot by forcing yourself to say what you want.

In Hollywood, nobody makes a movie until they have a clear idea what scene they're going to film first. But it is just as important for the filmmakers to know what they are going to film *last;* they need a complete plan from start to finish so they can gather the right people, equipment, and materials to shoot the movie as quickly and efficiently as possible. Like the big studio heads, you need a clear, distinct image of what your dream is so you can develop a plan to get there as quickly and efficiently as possible.

2. **When you write the script for your dream, start from the end and work your way backward.**
If you start writing your life script from where you are now, you might get distracted by the obstacles you think are in your way and never get to the fun part where you get to articulate your ultimate goal.

Suppose you want to become a doctor (we'll stay general here and leave researching how to become an endocrinologist up to you). By starting with your completed dream and working backward, the basic outline of your life script might look something like this:

5. Become a doctor.
4. Get accepted to and complete a residency program.
3. Graduate from medical school.
2. Get accepted to medical school.
1. Get good grades and take the right courses to increase chances of getting accepted into medical school.

Now let's look at how much more focused your script gets if you narrow the focus of your dream from just being "a doctor" to being a specific type of doctor, such as a heart surgeon.

6. Become a heart surgeon.
5. Do a cardiology residency at a hospital that specializes in heart surgery.
4. Graduate from a medical school with strong cardiology resources.
3. Get accepted into a medical school.
2. Research medical schools and find out which ones might offer the best guidance toward pursuing heart surgery.
1. Get good grades and take the right courses to increase chances of getting accepted into medical school.

Notice that both scripts lead to the same type of goal. However, if your real dream is to become a heart surgeon and you just follow the script to become a doctor, you'll get close to your dream, but you may not get as close to your dream as quickly as you should.

When you define a specific dream and make an outline of your script, you will not only identify the steps that will get you where you want to be, but you will clearly see the first steps you can take right now to start on your path.

No matter how big your dream may be, there's always something you can do right now to bring it one step closer to reality. So what are you waiting for? Your dream (and the rest of your life) is waiting.

 DIRECTOR'S NOTES: Every dream gives you a direction, but you need a script, or plan, that shows you exactly how to get there.

FOLLOW YOUR HEART

Efren

Long before anyone knew me as "Pedro" from *Napoleon Dynamite,* before you could see my face on T-shirts in Target and Wal-Mart, I remember getting dressed while memorizing my lines. I would put a large sweatshirt over my clothes and say good-bye to my parents. I had to walk down several blocks so I could catch the bus out of East L.A. through Glendale into Studio City, just so I could read for a part or go to the Samuel French bookstore right before going to my acting classes. Then I would take the bus back home. I remember sitting in the back of the bus with my Shakespeare book in my hand or a play or a scene for an audition, and being approached by homeboys asking me where I was from. I told them that I was an actor. They'd ask me what movies I had been in. I really hadn't done anything yet, and to that answer, they would say that I wasn't an actor.

At the time it was hard for me to hear that, but in retrospect, I was driven to do something that I loved. In some ways it was an escape; in some ways it was a way of expressing myself. I'd get home late at night and my mom would have saved dinner for me. They didn't understand really what I was doing but what they did know was that I was staying out of trouble, which made things easier for them.

Yes, I was tired. Yes, I had to read a lot. Yes, I had to know my way around Los Angeles. Yes, I had to have several jobs to not only help my parents make the rent, but to pay for my acting classes, my books, the bus, and my head shots. I took it as it came. I never thought about being a star. I hadn't thought about traveling the world. I studied the different techniques of acting out of curiosity and necessity. Acting cannot be taught, but the technique can be. The technique is there simply to get the actor connected in the moment, whatever that may be. The interesting thing is to look at a character in a moment, and to be in a moment, one has to accept the moment. And sometimes that is not easy.

I'd had a few small roles and was slowly building my "acting credits" while doing side jobs to pay the rent. But I was barely getting by.

Of course, when it rains, it pours—and one day I got drenched!

Like a one-two punch, my agent called and said I was being considered for two different movies. One was for a part in the Disney movie *The Alamo*, sharing the screen with big-name stars like Billy Bob Thornton and Dennis Quaid. It was a supporting role to be shot in Texas for about six weeks. This was a huge break for any actor.

And then there was the second one, a lead role in an independent, low-budget film starring actors that nobody had ever heard of. This second film would definitely not be considered an actor's big break.

But even though the role in *The Alamo* seemed the obvious choice, I read the script for the independent movie anyway. I wasn't looking for my big break; I wanted to find my greater challenge. The script for the independent film was different in style from what I had read before. Not only was the part bigger than the one in *The Alamo*, but it offered me an opportunity to take on a lead role.

The problem was choosing between a big studio picture as opposed to an independent film. The one would give me face time and maybe even a premiere and possibly a chance to meet more people who could further advance my career. The other would mean having either hot dogs or hamburgers for dinner—again.

My hardworking parents had sacrificed so much for the sake of the family, it was difficult to take on this independent film that was to shoot for 21 days without offering much. But I couldn't help it. It was a lead role in a movie, and that was important to me. I finally told my parents what I was thinking. I'll never forget what my father told me: *"Follow your heart."*

I felt silly for ever doubting my conscience. And so I accepted the part in the "smaller" picture, and that's when everything changed. You may have heard of this independent, low-budget movie called *Napoleon Dynamite*, which has gone on to make over $44 million in theaters and over $200 million in DVD and product sales. I was finally able to pay my parents back for all they'd done—by helping them to buy a house. In turn, I bought myself a house and started a production company with Chris and several other partners called Powerhouse Pictures Entertainment.

HOW I BECAME THE FIRST CORPORATE-SPONSORED COLLEGE STUDENT IN AMERICA

Chris

No dream, no idea is too crazy to pursue. I'm living proof. The summer before my senior year of high school, my friend Luke and I visited California from the East Coast to look at colleges. Our goal was to attend school on the West Coast for a change of scenery. We felt it would broaden our horizons, plus it would be great to live in warm weather year-round. After visiting top schools like the University of Southern California, Stanford, Pepperdine, and the University of California—Los Angeles, we got sticker shock at the cost of attending these colleges. All we could picture was years of student loans and then graduating with a crushing debt. The other option was to go to a local state university at home that cost one-third the price—but our dream was California.

One morning, while relaxing at the hotel before our next college tour, we saw Tiger Woods give a press conference on TV. He was wearing his Nike logo hat and talking about his latest golf tour. Luke and I looked at each other and said, "That's it! Why don't we get sponsored to go to college? We could wear the logo of a company 24/7 and become spokesguys for the company, which would allow them to reach out to a very lucrative market—college students!"

We had a plan. The next question was, "How can we convince a corporation to sponsor us?" That's when we got the crazy idea to advertise ourselves for sale on our own website called *www.chrisandluke.com.*

Within a week after we had returned home from the West Coast, we had our website up and running. It explained how we would advertise a company on our car, clothes, and surfboards. We had pictures stating we would eat a company's cereal, even if we weren't hungry, or fly in a company's planes, even if we didn't need to go anywhere.

Next, we designed custom T-shirts that read:

YOUR AD HERE

www.chrisandluke.com

Luke and I had no idea what would happen once we announced the site. Perhaps local media would think it was a good idea and interview us, but would national media respond?

To our amazement, within 24 hours of launching the story, morning rock radio shows began calling to interview us. What had started as just a "fun idea" was now becoming a reality. We told the radio hosts that we would be "spokesguys" for a company that was seeking to open or expand their college marketing. However, we would not be "spokesguys" for any company dealing with tobacco, sex, alcohol, or drugs. We wanted to make sure this was a mainstream campaign and one that could really help students.

Within a week, we had appeared on over 150 radio shows, and more were calling to book interviews with us. Then the local newspapers started requesting interviews and photo shoots. Once those stories ran, television stations started calling us. Soon we appeared on local TV shows on ABC, NBC, CBS, and Fox.

After the local media aired our story, the national shows and publications picked it up. As we were finishing our senior year in high school, national magazines like *People*, *TEEN*, *Cosmo Girl*, and others ran our story. Soon the business sections of Internet publications and national newspapers, like the *New York Post* and *USA Today*, pegged us as "Up and Comers to Watch!" Our typical days soon got very hectic. We'd wake up at 6:00 AM to do a live radio interview and then rush to school. We'd leave at lunch, do more interviews, and then rush back to school.

Then our story broke internationally. A French TV network sent a film crew to interview us, and soon a British and German film crew showed up as well. We even did a long-distance interview by telephone with a radio station in South Africa. The whole idea of two high school seniors being interviewed worldwide seemed so surreal.

In late March of our senior year, Luke and I knew we had to start making a decision about who would be our sponsor. Initially, we thought we would have to reach out to companies to "pitch" ourselves, but in a matter of a few months, because of all the media attention, over 20 companies, both large and small, had called us, including AT&T and HotJobs. But we felt the right deal had not yet come along. Then one morning, we received a call from First USA in Wilmington, Delaware, a Division of Bank One in Chicago. Their marketing department explained that they had read about us in

People magazine and someone from their corporate offices in Chicago had forwarded our website for review. They were intrigued with our concept, as they were developing a national college program about student financial responsibility. This was sounding good.

They further explained that we would *not* be selling credit cards to students but instead teaching students how to be fiscally responsible. We knew that many students entered college with their first credit card in hand. To many, it meant free cash. They'd purchase stuff like cell phones, big-screen TVs, and stereo equipment, only to be shocked when the bills arrived by the realization that they had no way to pay it all back.

Luke and I really liked the idea of helping students learn to be financially responsible. We also liked that we wouldn't have to sell a product. We met with the First USA marketing team. They were all young, recent college graduates who related to us and our goals. Within two weeks, we signed the deal. For maximum impact, we decided to announce our sponsor live on *The Today Show* on the morning of our high school graduation.

We spent the next few weeks in bank and media training to become knowledgeable about every aspect of the bank and its student financial responsibility program. The bank bought us shorts, pants, shirts, and caps with its logo on it, along with coffee mugs for our dorm rooms. It even flew us to Chicago to have a private lunch with James Dimon, CEO of Bank One.

When graduation day arrived, *The Today Show* sent a Town Car and driver to take us to the show so we could arrive by 7:00 AM. We arrived at Rockefeller Center, where Al Roker greeted us as he chatted with the crowd all around. Security escorted us into the NBC studios and took us to the green room, the waiting area for guests before they appear on the show. Luke and I rushed to eat the free bagels, muffins, fruit, cheese, coffee, and juices that NBC provided for all of its guests.

Although we weren't nervous about our appearance, the bank marketing team that came along with us seemed very tense. This would be the first time their bank would be featured on the number one morning show in America, viewed by millions, so they kept reviewing with us the points they wanted us to emphasize about their bank. Joe Rogan, host of the TV show *Fear Factor*, was also on the show that morning. He, too, noticed how nervous the marketing team was and smiled at Luke and me. Just think, a few short months ago we were in California, worried about how we could possibly pay for college, and now here we were eating bagels with Joe Rogan, about to appear on national TV.

We got situated on the set. Ann Curry, who was conducting the interview, walked on the set and greeted Luke and me. Then we heard "in 5-4-3-2-1," and we were live! After a brief introduction, Ann turned to us and said, "Okay, who is the sponsor?"

Luke lifted his shirt, revealing the bank's logo on a shirt underneath, and I said, "We are thrilled to be sponsored by First USA." Later, we found out that the bank marketing team screamed with joy in the green room as we made that announcement! We explained that our corporate sponsorship deal consisted of our full college tuition, approximately $40,000 a year each, $3,000 per semester for expenses, clothes with their bank logo, and surfboards also with their logo. Then we announced that Luke was attending the University of Southern California in Los Angeles and I would be attending Pepperdine University in Malibu.

The segment flew by very quickly, and during the commercial break, we met Matt Lauer and Al Roker. Back in the green room, the bank marketing team congratulated us, and a Town Car took us back home to prepare for our high school graduation.

Our graduation appeared on TV news shows across the country. By 10:00 PM that same night, we had to go back to New York City to prepare for a national satellite media tour early the next morning. We also appeared live on CNN and some local New York City television shows. Within 48 hours of our corporate sponsorship announcement, we had given First USA 50 million media impressions in the form of television, newspaper, and magazine appearances.

That August, CNN, MSNBC, KTLA, and other TV news crews followed us to film two guys from New Jersey, the very first corporately sponsored college students in America, moving into their dorms. Over the next few months, we spoke to college students about financial responsibility. We received a call from *People* alerting us that we had been chosen to be in their year-end issue of "The 25 Most Intriguing People of 2001." And to think, this all began with nothing more than two high school students trying to find a way to pay for college. We'd had a dream, and perhaps at the time it was a crazy dream, but we had followed though and made it a reality.

Don't be afraid of pursuing your crazy dream—you never know, it can actually come true!

PRODUCTION ASSISTANT'S TASKS

☆ Ask yourself what you enjoy doing.
Make a list of your hobbies and interests and think
about ways to do them more often and with more
commitment. Be as specific as possible.

☆ Open your eyes and look at everyone
around you.
How do they live their lives? Is there anyone—a
member of your family, an acquaintance or colleague,
a famous person—whom you think has it all figured
out? What does that person spend her time doing?
Research the lives you are interested in—ask questions, go to Wikipedia, read biographies . . . do whatever it takes to find out as much as you can.

☆ Turn up your imagination.
Be curious; ask questions. Think of the most prepos-
terous ideas you can. Make a list of your "crazy ideas,"
being as specific as you can be.

☆ Make a "step list."
Start with a goal at the top, then work backward
to where you are now.

☆ Talk to people about your goal and the steps
to get there.
If it sounds exciting and possible as you say it out
loud, you might just have the idea for your life script
on your hands!

CHAPTER 2

Edit Your Life Script

Okay, so you've written a rough draft of your life script. How does it look? Before you start down your path, you must realize that like any Hollywood script, your life script may need a little editing.

Are you sure this is the dream you want to commit yourself to? Are you sure you know how to get there? If you're going to bring your dream into focus, you've got to make sure you pick the right one. We both struggled to pick ours, and we're going to show you exactly how to do it.

The Right Dream Points You in the Right Direction

On a piece of paper, draw a circle. Put an X anywhere outside that circle, and put a dot anywhere inside it. That dot represents you, and the X represents your perfect dream.

Now put the tip of a pencil on the dot, close your eyes, spin the paper around, and with your eyes still closed, try to draw a line from the dot to the *X*. Do this several times. The chances are good that you'll miss the *X* every time, and that's what you'll do if you metaphorically "close your eyes" and live your life without deciding to pursue a specific dream. You may get lucky and hit the jackpot, but odds are that you'll never achieve your dream life unless you know what it is and how to develop a plan to get it.

> CHRIS: Just as it takes time to bring a shot into focus with a camera, it takes a bit of time to zoom in on an ambition that is right for you. And sometimes the people around you will recognize that you are living your dream before you do. This is because doing what you love surrounds you with a positive energy that's obvious to others.

Here's how most people pick the wrong dream:

- They focus on the rewards.
- They do what's easy and convenient.
- They do what other people tell them to do.
- They restrict themselves to dreams they think are easy to achieve.
- They don't discover which dream they really want to pursue.

 DIRECTOR'S NOTES: To make a plan, you need to make sure you have chosen the right dream.

Don't Focus on Rewards

It's fun to focus on the rewards of any dream. Everyone likes to fantasize about what it would be like to become a movie star, business owner, or supermodel. While there's nothing wrong with fantasizing, there's a big difference between fantasy and actual dreams. Simply put, daydreaming isn't dreaming.

With fantasies, you only focus on the rewards. Doing this is like walking through a forest and looking only at the birds in the trees above you — if you are constantly looking above and ahead, you're likely to trip over what's right in front of you. A person who is focused on rewards tends to jump from one goal to another. First he might want to be an actor. When that's too hard, he might try becoming a singer. When that becomes too hard, he tries something else. He winds up spending so much time searching for the easiest path to riches, that all the time is wasted — he never finds his true dream.

EFREN: At first, my parents didn't really understand why I got on the bus every day to get to acting classes on top of school and my job. They were
just happy that I was staying out of trouble. But
when they saw me in commercials, they were proud
of my achievements.

With dreams, you focus on the activity. If you truly want to sing — notice we didn't say "be a singer" — then you'll have to learn to sing and practice singing whenever you can. Any rewards you earn as a singer, such as fame and money, should be thought of as bonuses on top of your real reward—having the opportunity to sing. If you focus on the activity you want to do, you'll always have the reward of doing something that makes you feel happy and fulfilled. If you only focus on the imagined rewards, you'll most likely end up with nothing.

Remember, success is never a destination. True success always lies in the journey. If you don't enjoy the journey you choose, you'll never last long enough on that journey to get any of the potential rewards.

 DIRECTOR'S NOTES: If you focus on the activity you want to do, you'll always have the reward of doing something you love.

Don't Take the Easy Way Out

People who only want rewards also want them as quickly and easily as possible. As a result, these people are suckers for every get-rich-quick idea that comes their way. Imagine someone who thinks being a movie star is a fast track to riches, so she wants to try to become an actor. The second she realizes that acting takes time, work, and dedication, she'll jump ship and find another way to make money in a hurry. Maybe she'll try becoming a model, but when she finds out that, too, takes time, work, and dedication, she'll bail out of that dream and find another that promises an easier and faster route to success.

Don't let this happen to you. The real secret is that the easiest and fastest way to any kind of reward is to pick the dream you truly want, regardless of whether you think it will be easy, make you a lot of money, or make you famous. Don't be afraid to chase after the biggest dream you can think of. What makes any dream achievable is simply your own interest in it.

However, just because you are interested in something doesn't mean that your path toward success will be easy. In fact, struggle and hard work constitute the journey. But if you choose something to pursue that you find fun and fulfilling, the work will seem less strenuous than if you are pushing against your own sensibilities to reach a goal that is not your true calling.

If you have little interest in singing, you'll have a difficult time becoming a singer, because you won't be able to commit yourself to doing breathing exercises every day. If you don't care about acting, then spending time going out on auditions and taking acting classes will seem unbearable. If you hate to cook, you may never get through that first class, and that dream of hosting your own cooking show on TV will fly out the window. Whatever you find difficult, someone else will find fun. Fortunately, it works the other way around—what others find difficult, you'll find fun.

Everyone is born with certain skills, but talent is only useful if you use it to pursue a dream that you really want. If you have a passion for singing, you'll eventually develop even the tiniest bit of talent into something extraordinary through constant and consistent practice. All the hard work will seem easy compared to trying to force yourself to participate in activities you dislike just for the fame and fortune. Remember, no dream is "easy" to achieve. When the going gets tough, only your passion will carry you through.

 DIRECTOR'S NOTES: The easiest and fastest way to any reward is to pick the dream you truly want.

Maintain the Integrity of Your Life Script

Every movie script is read by other people—agents, development executives, producers, directors, actors—and each of these people has an opinion about it. Although edits and compromises are made, the person responsible for maintaining the script's integrity and vision is the screenwriter. Because you are the author of your own life script, you must protect your vision. You will receive a lot of feedback from critics. Listen to the comments, but remember: you're in charge of the script.

Most people who give you advice are trying to help you, and sometimes they are helpful. Friends and family members and even complete strangers can offer a fresh perspective on your situation, because they can examine you objectively. They may recognize talents and skills that you might take for granted or even ignore altogether. For example, if your friends and family members constantly tell you that you have a knack for fixing things, this might help you identify the seed of your dream to become a mechanic. Or if a total stranger compliments your speaking voice, you might consider becoming a professional speaker. No matter what is particularly unique and special about you, other people can often recognize it and bring it to your attention.

> CHRIS: At Sundance, I met two filmmakers, and we became friends. After hanging out during the festival and hearing my story, they picked up on my public relations skills and asked me to help them promote their film. Until they said it, I hadn't thought of promoting films other than the one I had been in. I've been doing it ever since, thanks to their suggestion!

But there's a problem with listening to other people: not everyone has your best interests at heart. Your parents, though they love and support you and say they have your best interests in mind, may tell you to go to school to become a doctor or a lawyer even though you have a passion for photography. They may encourage you to do something other than your dream job because they want a secure future for you, as most parents want for their children, no matter the age of their children.

If you take their advice and start taking organic chemistry classes, you might be able to get decent grades, but if you're nagged by thoughts of exploring the Amazon rain forest and taking pictures of endangered wildlife, then you should probably be in the photography class down the hall. Talk to your parents and explain your dream and your plan. The more convinced you are that it will happen, the more they will be able to begin to change their view of your future. They might even see that urging you to seek a career solely for a sense of security will only get in the way of your success. Just think of how proud they'll be when one of your photos makes the cover of *National Geographic*.

This change will only come through your dedication to your dream. It won't happen during the course of one conversation, but it will happen eventually though your hard work and adherence to your life script. Your parents might even get into it and offer support and suggestions for moving toward *your* goal—not theirs. But along the way, you will receive input from all kinds of people, whether you want it or not. Here are some strategies to help you deal with other people's "advice":

- *Listen to what they have to say.* Be polite and open—you never know what someone is going to say, and that person might come up with some good ideas, especially if you are still brainstorming.
- *Ask questions.* Why does he think what he thinks? What is she basing her advice on? Sometimes the person will have valid reasons for the suggestion. If you love to play with your niece and nephew at family get-togethers, your family may suggest that you go into child care or teaching. Whether you are interested in these fields or not, they are at least basing their comments on something that you truly

enjoy. But if someone tells you to pursue a dream but can't explain why you should (beyond saying that it would be a "safe" or "secure" career), then you know that this person may be speaking out of fear rather than hope and drive.

- *Listen to the explanation, then listen to yourself.* While he is explaining his motivations, be aware of your reactions. Are you excited by what he suggests? Repelled? Angered? Confused? These feelings will help you articulate to him and to yourself why you can or cannot choose to go in whatever direction he is suggesting.

- *Explain your position.* Look at this encounter as an opportunity to test your dream out on others. Describe the classes you'll take, the job opportunities, and the adventures associated with your passion. The more specific, the better.

- *See if anything she is saying may help you with your goal.* Sometimes others can help you nail down some specifics of your plan. For example, if you are describing your plan to become a photographer, your mom might offer you her old camera or get you in touch with a friend of hers who shoots for the *Washington Post.* You never know what could come out of this type of exchange of ideas; parents and friends want to help, and they will feel as though they have if you allow them into your plan.

- *Continue on your path.* If someone suggests you pursue something that you know won't make you happy, you have two choices. You can listen and follow a dream that will leave you feeling empty and unsatisfied inside; or you can thank the other person for the advice, try to understand why that person is telling you to pursue a particular dream, and then choose to incorporate some of the advice into finding what you really want. Choosing the first path is guaranteed to steer you away from happiness, while choosing the second path gives you the advantage of listening to others and the freedom to choose your own way. Which choice do you want to make?

☆ **DIRECTOR'S NOTES:** Although edits and compromises are made, the only person responsible for maintaining the script's integrity and vision is the screenwriter. Because you are the author of your own life script, you must protect your vision.

Don't Settle for a Lesser Dream

It's a real tragedy when someone settles for a "small" dream because he doesn't believe he can reach his bigger dream. When you settle for less, you will never achieve any sense of satisfaction or accomplishment, because you're shortchanging yourself out of your true desires. To go for a dream of any size, you must believe that you deserve to pursue it.

EFREN: When I decided to take the role in *Napoleon Dynamite*, I had another offer for a smaller role in a bigger movie. But I knew that I needed to take bigger roles in smaller films to get where I wanted to be.

Imagine a movie director wrapping a shoot mid-production by telling the camera crew and actors, "Hey, I don't deserve to make a major Hollywood blockbuster. Let's just play it safe, take home what we already have, and just make a short film instead." Needless to say, this director would be fired by the studio. You are the director of your own life, but you have to be the studio head, the producers, the crew, and the actors, too. If you think that you don't deserve the biggest, brightest, most exciting dream possible, then fire the director in your mind who's telling you to call it quits, and replace her with a more driven director who will get you where you want to go.

 DIRECTOR'S NOTES: By settling for a lesser dream, you will never achieve any sense of satisfaction or accomplishment.

Don't Choose Too Many Dreams

Sometimes you may not have just one dream, but several. Maybe you want to climb Mount Everest, design your own line of cosmetics, become a concert pianist, win the Miss

America Pageant, and write and publish a novel. Though a tad ambitious, it is possible to do all of those things, but you can't do them all at once; you need to know which dream you want the most and focus on that one. Once you accomplish that one, you can move on to the next project.

If you find yourself overwhelmed by too many dreams, write down each one on a piece of paper and grade each dream with an *A, B,* or *C.* An *A* dream is one that you absolutely must pursue. A *B* dream is one that you want to pursue but not at the expense of giving up any of your *A* dreams. A *C* dream would be nice to pursue, but you don't mind setting it aside temporarily.

After grading your dreams, see how many *B* and *C* dreams you can eliminate completely. Some dreams may just be fantasies—sure, starting a cosmetics line or competing in the Miss America pageant would be fun, but what is your motivation and how have you prepared? If you want to have a business or a Miss America tiara but aren't interested in the actions associated with obtaining these items—pouring time and money into getting the business off the ground or striding across a stage in a bikini—you might be talking about fantasies, not concrete dreams. By taking action, you can turn any fantasy into a dream, but if you don't really want to do those actions, then eliminate "Become Miss America" from your list of dreams.

CHRIS: When I agreed to be in *The Corporation,* I never thought it would win an award at Sundance. Being in an award-winning film and my subsequent

career in the film industry was a happy accident
that grew out of my original dream of going to
college.

Some goals may involve more of a commitment in an area that you don't truly enjoy. Are you really willing to go through the years of mental and physical workouts and practices that will get you to the top of Mount Everest if you don't even make the effort to get to pilates class once a week? Cross "Climb Mount Everest" off the list.

Next, try to group similar dreams together. If "Become a world-renowned chef" and "Open my own five-star restaurant" are on your list, you're in luck. These two dreams are complementary. To achieve both, you'll need to master skills that are related, such as the history of French cuisine and how to manage a small business. Your dream of owning your own restaurant can grow out of your dream of becoming a chef, so you'll essentially pursue both dreams one after another.

On the other hand, sometimes your dreams may conflict with each other. If you want to start your own Internet company selling antiques and collectibles, you might not have time to pursue another dream of working for an organization dedicated to stopping the genocide in Darfur. If two unrelated dreams appear on your list, you need to decide which of the two is more important to you.

In Hollywood, a director may have a dozen screenplays that he thinks would make wonderful movies, but he can only make one of them at a time. From a list of multiple dreams, boil down your list to the one *A* dream that's most important to you, the script that must get done first. If you find two dreams equally important, try to find a way to make them coexist. You can do anything, but you still need to decide what's most important in the long run. If you chase too many dreams, you may never have time to achieve any of them.

 DIRECTOR'S NOTES: You can achieve everything you want, but you can't always do it all at the same time.

HOW I RECOGNIZED MY DREAM

Efren

My dream of acting began early in high school when I was involved in many school productions, including *Oklahoma!*, *West Side Story*, *The Odd Couple*, *Paint Your Wagon*, and *Blow, Gabriel, Blow*. Even though some plays were musicals and some were comedies or dramas, I found that I enjoyed performing in each play just for the chance to be creative.

Thankfully, my parents never tried to force my brothers or me to do anything we didn't want to do, and they encouraged us to explore and find our own dreams. My older brother, Cesar, the brawn in the family, was always fascinated with the military and joined the Marines. My other brother, Eddie, enjoyed studying history and wound up attending the University of Southern California to study philosophy and political science. My brother Julio enjoys drafting and mechanical engineering and has made a career out of it. My brother Julian is a photographer and enjoys composing music. My twin brother, Carlos, is studying acting.

I grew up loving stories and poetry. I loved having the ability to tell a story on stage through someone else's words. The idea of spending my life acting captivated me, because it let me create a character and express my own interpretation of the material.

I remember when I got the part of Linus in my high school's production of *You're a Good Man, Charlie Brown*. I spent all my free time memorizing my lines and hoping that when the play opened, I wouldn't mess up. We practiced and rehearsed every day. Although I had to learn a lot of lines, the process wasn't hard in a negative way but instead was challenging and exciting. Before, I had never thought of acting as a goal; I just knew that I enjoyed doing it. I learned one scene at a time and was thrilled as the production and cast slowly came together.

Then the whole thing fell apart.

A week before we opened, half the cast and crew walked out. Some had schedule conflicts, others decided they were just too busy to participate, and still others were just exhausted and couldn't go on. Despite the fact that I wanted to stay, the show was cancelled. I couldn't put on a one-man show.

Although the production was cancelled, through the time spent rehearsing, I had realized that I was able to create my own voice on stage and have it heard. From that experience, I learned teamwork, honesty to myself and others, time management, and how other people work. More importantly,

I learned that it's easy to pursue a goal when everything's going your way, but when adversity hits and the world seems to fall apart around you, that's the time to ask yourself what you really want to do. If you're willing to stick to your dream despite massive setbacks, you'll know in your heart what you truly want to do.

REWARDS ARE RECEIVED IN RETROSPECT

Chris

After we secured corporate sponsorship to attend college, Luke and I were thrilled with our success. We were at the colleges of our dreams, and we were helping young people learn about financial responsibility. Going to college for free had been the original goal, but on top of that, a whole world of opportunities opened up to us beyond credit cards and classrooms.

One of the highlights of our success was being interviewed by the media. I never lost my excitement for sharing my sponsorship news every chance I got. When you are doing something you find fun and exciting, you'll find you have a naturally positive energy about you. Most of the time, other people will notice this before you do, and magazines and other press will want to investigate you because your outlook will give them a story that could inspire others. So it wasn't surprising when newspapers and magazines wanted to interview me for stories, but it did surprise me when I received an offer to appear in a documentary film.

When my publicist called to tell me about a documentary interview request, I agreed to do it without much thought. I was told that the film, called *The Corporation*, was a documentary for Canadian television about American corporations, and its producers were interested in my story. I knew it was important to seize every opportunity, no matter how small it might seem, because sharing success is the only way to attract more.

After the interview, I didn't hear anything about the film until a year later, when the producers told me the film was going to premiere at the 2003 Toronto Film Festival and the filmmakers wanted my media reel to fill out my section of the film. I sent the producers VHS copies of the appearances and was excited that the film would be seen by an audience. I was lucky enough to attend the film's premiere in Toronto, and I was completely shocked at what I saw. The film received a standing ovation and was the second runner-up for the festival's AGF People's Choice Award. I never imagined that one little interview could turn into this kind of attention.

Soon after the Toronto Film Festival, *The Corporation* was accepted into the 2004 Sundance Film Festival. I didn't want to miss a chance to go to the biggest American film festival, so I started planning my first trip to Sundance the moment I learned that the film would be making its U.S. premiere there. Sundance turned out to be one of the best events of my life, a huge meeting of the minds that introduced me to so much talent and so many opportunities. That's when I learned that when you're chasing your dream, never say no to an opportunity, no matter how small it seems. Becoming involved in a project without worrying whether or not it will give you huge rewards is the only way you can put yourself out there so the rewards can find you in the first place. To think I owed it all to a documentary that I thought would only appear on Canadian TV.

PRODUCTION ASSISTANT'S TASKS

☆ Separate your dreams from your fantasies.
Make a list of everything you'd like to accomplish and grade each according to importance. Your *A* dreams are the ones you should investigate first.

☆ Strategize.
If you have more than one *A* dream in your life script, brainstorm about how to accomplish them simultaneously. Although this is rarely doable, it is possible with careful thought and planning.

☆ Stay focused.
Don't bounce from one dream to another, looking for the easy way out. Dreams are hard to achieve, but if you're pursuing the right one, the work won't seem like work at all.

☆ Practice explaining your dream to other people.
If they have different ideas about what you should do, listen politely, then explain your dream and see if any of their advice can be incorporated into your plans.

☆ Dream big.
Don't settle for "small" dreams because you are scared or intimidated. Push yourself to imagine yourself accomplishing everything your life script details. Go back to your script and add bigger and better ideas. The more comfortable you become with the possibilities of a life lived through passion, the easier living that life will become.

CHAPTER 3

Let Fun Unlock
Your Creativity

Once a script is written and edited, it's time to pitch it. And no studio buys a script that is pitched to them by a writer or director who isn't enthusiastic about his project. Now that you've got your life script down, get enthused—have some fun.

Your capacity to have fun is key to making your dream a reality. It's not just the amount of talent or intelligence you might have that will create your success but how your talent and intelligence is applied. And the best way to apply yourself is to have fun.

CHRIS: At my first Sundance film festival, I found myself face-to-face with some of North America's most notable film stars. I easily could have felt intimidated. But once I realized how much fun everyone was having, I knew the best way to connect with these people was to do as they did and let myself have fun, too. By opening myself up to having a good time, I got to become friends with some of the most famous actors in the world.

All successful people enjoy what they're doing. We certainly do! But think of Bill Gates, Oprah Winfrey, Steven Spielberg, or Julia Roberts. Can you imagine Steven Spielberg grumbling to his wife that he has to make another movie this year? Do you think Oprah Winfrey complains to her friends that hosting her own talk show on TV is just too much work and that she deserves more days off? How often do you think Bill Gates and Julia Roberts stare out of the window, wishing they had chosen another line of work? Remember, being famous isn't the goal. The goal is to use publicity and fame to help you reach your dreams, and the best way to become famous is to do something you love doing anyway. After all, when was the last time anyone got famous by complaining about her job?

Turn Obstacles into Opportunities

Here's a myth about success: too many people think that if only they can reach a certain goal, their lives will be stress-free and problem-free forever. The truth is that problems are part of everyone's life. We certainly know it personally. Even Oprah Winfrey and Steven Spielberg run into problems every day. Trying to avoid problems, or believing that you can reach a point in life when you no longer have any problems, is like running outside in a thunderstorm and trying to dodge the raindrops. You may be able to avoid some of them, but you'll never be able to avoid all of them.

Although you can't avoid problems, you can change how you handle them. As you may imagine, if you lose your temper, it won't get you any closer to your goals. A more useful solution is to control your anger and look at problems as opportunities. If you see problems as obstacles, they'll always keep you from reaching your goals. If you see them as opportunities, you can use them as stepping stones to bring you one step closer to your dreams.

During a movie shoot, problems pop up all the time. It may be sunny out when the director wants it to be cloudy and overcast. Sometimes actors don't show up, lights burn out, cameras break, or airplanes suddenly fly overhead making it impossible to hear the actors speak. Instead of getting upset, a good director can use these problems as an opportunity for additional rehearsals or to experiment with different ways of filming a scene.

For example, on the set of the first Indiana Jones movie, *Raiders of the Lost Ark,* Harrison Ford was supposed to fight a long, drawn-out, choreographed battle in a marketplace with a machete-wielding attacker. Unfortunately, that day Ford was battling an illness and barely had the strength to show up on the set, let alone spend the next few hours in a mock life-and-death battle. So instead of filming the scene as written, Ford suggested that when his attacker first challenges him, he could just pull out his pistol and shoot him. That's the scene they filmed, it turned out to be one of the most comical and memorable scenes of the entire movie, and it would never have happened if Ford hadn't gotten sick.

EFREN: On the set of *Napoleon Dynamite*, we ran into delays and obstacles almost every day of shooting. But whenever my scene was delayed, I'd sit and go over my lines, my character's motivations. When it came time to perform, I felt more prepared and connected to the moment. So I owe some of my performance to the delays on set!

As you move along with your life script, count on encountering obstacles. Look for ways to have fun with any problem that might come up. For example, say you have taken your first step toward becoming a writer and settled on a name for your new, brilliant blog: WriteRight. Good first step. Then you Google the name only to find out that the domain name is already taken by a mysterious company that offers a "program to help people deliver the written word effectively."

At this point, you have two options: one, forget about starting a blog altogether, or two, look at it as a great time to exercise your imagination brainstorming new blog names with friends. A person who chooses the first option is creating more of a problem than truly exists, while a person who grabs a pen and a notebook and starts writing down new ideas will most likely come up with an even better name for the project and move along toward his dream.

 DIRECTOR'S NOTES: "Problems" can be opportunities in disguise.

Increase Your Chances
of Success

Let's be honest: Not everything that will happen as you move toward achieving your goal will be inherently fun. Realizing that someone already holds the domain name for your new blog is not fun. Getting sick on the set of a film is not fun. Being stuck in a hideous traffic jam on your way to a job interview is not fun. But with the right attitude and a dash of creativity, you have the power to inject fun into these types of situations.

For example, imagine that two people heading to the same marketing job interview both get stuck in rush hour traffic. One person gets upset, screams at other drivers, and fumes as traffic crawls along. The other person uses the time to focus on her dreams. She rehearses what she might say to her interviewer and thinks about how she wants to present herself. As she thinks things over, she starts to have fun coming up with ideas about how her potential employer could use rush hour traffic to help promote and market various products to people stuck in their cars.

Maybe the company could hand out free samples to people stopped at red lights. Or it could hire a truck (with an advertiser's name prominently displayed) to haul around a video screen that plays a popular TV show that people in rush hour could watch while receiving an audio broadcast through their car radios. Or maybe it could pay the tolls of commuters for a day to speed up traffic and give people a reason to associate speed and convenience with the sponsoring company. As she brainstorms, the second job candidate builds confidence and enthusiasm that will show through in her interview (assuming traffic starts moving and she gets there on time). And who knows, she may have come up with just the idea the company has been looking for, all because of a traffic jam.

> EFREN: Upon leaving Preston, Idaho, after the *Napoleon Dynamite* shoot, a guy gave me his Preston High School T-shirt, which says on the back, "It's not the hours you put in. It's what you put into those hours."

Fun is contagious. Having fun with any situation not only makes life more enjoyable, but it often increases the chances that you'll reach your dream much faster, as well. Everyone wants to have fun, and everyone wants to be around others who can help them have fun. The more fun you have, the more people you'll attract who will want to help you reach your dream. The bottom line is this: You literally can't afford not to have fun. If you're not having fun, you're doing something wrong. If you're having fun and progressing toward your goals, then you're doing something right.

Tyler Hinman knows how this works. In 1998, at the age of 14, Hinman did his first *New York Times* crossword puzzle. At first, he did it for the fun of the challenge. Then he discovered crossword puzzle tournaments. Figuring he'd have even more fun, he entered his first tournament in 2001 and came in 101st place—a pretty good ranking given that hundreds of people of all ages participated. But even though he did well, Hinman had his heart set on higher goals: he realized that if he could win the American Crossword Puzzle Tournament before 2008, he could become the youngest crossword puzzle champion in tournament history.

Faced with this challenge, he put his dream into action by practicing several crossword puzzles every day. Gradually he learned the common crossword puzzle clues and answers and how to interpret particularly tricky clues. He soon found that the Monday *New York Times* crossword puzzles were the easiest, but it took him a month before he could complete a Tuesday crossword puzzle. Then it took him another year before he could consistently complete a Friday crossword puzzle. Day by day, he kept honing his skills and practicing. At his next tournament, he came in 64th; then the following year, he came in 19th. Finally, he reached 12th place, and then, three years before his deadline of 2008, he became the youngest crossword puzzle champion in history. Hinman succeeded because he believed in himself, took action to improve his craft, and most importantly, had a blast while doing it. Hinman literally played all day to reach his dream. And that's what you can do, too.

 DIRECTOR'S NOTES: Having fun not only makes life more enjoyable but increases the chances that you'll reach your dream much more quickly.

Use Fun to Make Things Happen

Most people have life backward. They think that the only way to succeed is to step on others and claw their way to the top. Those people may achieve temporary success, but they may never feel satisfied or secure. Often they can't even enjoy their success. But if you focus on making yourself happy, you'll in turn make others happy. The ultimate way to use the fun you'll have while pursuing your goal is to figure out a way to solve a problem. The truth is that if you can help others, you'll always help yourself.

> CHRIS: When Luke and I came up with our idea to be sponsored by a corporation, we wanted to choose the right corporation so we could use the project as a way to help people. In the end, we used the opportunity to help college students understand fiscal responsibility, which was very rewarding.

Here are the basic steps to making things happen by having fun:

1. *Find a way to have fun.* As we said before, if you aren't having fun, you're doing something wrong.
2. *Think of a problem.* Can you solve it by using your passion in some way?
3. *Publicize yourself and your actions so others will want to be part of your dream.* You may be the smartest engineer or most talented choreographer in the world, but how can anyone hire or help you if they don't even know you exist?

Suppose you want to start your own company. First, you'll have to find something that you'll enjoy doing just because it's fun. That way, even if your idea goes nowhere, you'll still have had fun and learned some valuable skills and lessons that you can apply in the future. For example, you might love playing Second Life and learning about virtual reality. Let's think that through using the steps outlined above.

1. *If virtual reality is fun for you,* you're ready for Step 2.
2. *Ask yourself who might benefit from virtual reality.* Architectural firms? Maybe you could design virtual worlds from their plans so clients could "walk" through a building before it's been built. Real estate companies? Maybe you could create virtual versions of homes for sale so buyers could experience a home before physically visiting it. Hospitals? Maybe you could create virtual images of a human body so doctors could practice surgical procedures before operating on a real patient. Choose whatever you think will be the most fun for you. In any job or business, the key isn't how much you know but how much you can help others. The more you can help others, the closer you'll get to success.
3. *Make yourself known to others.* Nobody can reach a dream without the help of other people. Find a unique way to promote yourself. Start a website or blog, issue press releases to your local newspaper and TV stations, or volunteer your time and services for a charity event. Attract the attention of people who can help you.

The trick to turning your fun into success is to find a way to include or help other people. To make your talent and intelligence work for you, you need to have fun, let others know you're having fun, and find a way to make having fun beneficial for anyone capable of helping you. When Chris started his website asking for corporate sponsors to pay for college, he was having fun. When Efren chose the role of Pedro in *Napoleon Dynamite*, he wanted to experience the fun of playing a bigger role than he had played before. We both moved toward things we thought would be fun — and we both had success.

 DIRECTOR'S NOTES: Having fun guarantees that no matter what happens, you'll enjoy the process.

HAVING FUN CAN SET YOU FREE
Efren

As an actor, I don't know what's more frightening: being on stage or being on stage and not knowing what's going to happen next. At one of my first acting schools, The Young Actors Space, I learned something called improvisation. Improv is a form of acting where the actor is placed in a situation without a script and forced to make everything up. Sometimes we'd have to play the scene dramatically, and other times we'd play the scene as a farce. Sometimes we'd even act out an entire scene while speaking in gibberish.

When I tried to explain improv to people who asked me about acting school, the more I tried, the less sense it would make. It might not make sense logically, but creatively it does. Working without the security blanket of a script gives actors the freedom to let go of their preconceived thoughts and to trust their own imaginations. This freedom allows actors to listen, react, and respond to others more organically.

Improv is terrifying, frightening, frustrating, and ultimately fun. Being thrown into a situation on stage where I didn't know what would happen next made me realize how little I knew about acting. However, the more I practiced letting go, experimenting and failing, and allowing myself to crash and burn, the stronger I got as an actor.

Some of my classmates got frustrated with improv and dropped out of the class, while others fought the process and failed to learn as much as they could have. Even though learning how to improvise was challenging, I stuck with it and learned a tremendous amount about acting. I was willing to trust my instincts—and I had fun doing it. Whenever I find myself facing a challenge, I don't let it discourage me. We are always going to be confronted with obstacles. It's how we approach them that determines the outcome.

HAVING FUN CAN OPEN DOORS
Chris

Being successful isn't just about whom you know; it's how you meet them. The way you meet someone can tell you what kind of role that person might play in your future—whether the two of you will just become good friends, or if you'll do that and combine your talents to work on a shared project. Meeting people in the film industry and networking to form contacts might seem uptight and intimidating, but I've been lucky enough to have met some of the most influential and talented people in the film world—all while having a good time.

In 2004, I got the chance to attend the Sundance Film Festival where *The Corporation*, was making its U.S. premiere. As soon as I arrived in Park City, Utah, I could already feel the excitement of the festival building up. I was a little nervous when I arrived since I didn't know anyone. However, I was pleasantly surprised to find that everyone was just focused on having a great time and meeting new people. I felt relaxed right away, and even though the mountain air was freezing cold, the excitement from the festival kept everyone nice and warm.

At the first screening of *The Corporation*, I met the film-makers at the theater, and the director gave me an official Sundance filmmaker badge. Then I got the wonderful opportunity to meet some other people who were in the film. Ironically, a lot of people who are in the very same documentary, or even the same feature film, don't actually get to meet each other until the film premiere. Meeting everyone made me feel a part of something that was big and real. It was exciting to see the wonderful reception we received—a standing ovation at the end of the first screening. The stars of the film were invited to the front of the theater to answer questions, and the director, Mark Achbar, introduced us to the crowd. It was an unbelievable feeling and a privilege to answer all of the interesting questions the audience had for us. After the screening, a filmgoer even asked me to sign her Sundance Film Festival program.

The Corporation ended up winning the World Cinema Documentary Audience Award. I remember at the party after the awards, a filmmaker came up and congratulated me. That moment made me realize that I was headed in the right direction and surrounding myself with the right people.

Besides meeting people in my own film, I also met an actress, Vanessa Bauche, who appeared in another Canadian film called *A Silent Love*. We just happened to be sitting near each other at a world cinema party, and since we were both in Canadian films, we had a lot in common. We became friends at the festival, and she invited me to her film's premiere. The film was amazing, and I got to go out to dinner with Vanessa, the producers, and the director. I didn't even realize that Vanessa had also starred in one of my all-time favorite foreign films, Alejandro González Iñárritu's *Amores Perros*, until later that night. Meeting Vanessa was such a great experience because I met her while we were at a party having fun. When people are enjoying themselves and celebrating their own work, it is surprisingly easy to forge new friendships and make new connections.

The final night of the festival, actor Thomas Ian Nicholas and his brother, Tim Scarne, were crashing at the same house where I was spending the night. They had a small film called *LA DJ* that wasn't being shown at Sundance, but they had decided to come out anyway to network and have a good time. I spoke with Tim and Thom and they were telling me about their film and got me really interested in it. I had been a fan of Thom's first film, *Rookie of the Year*, as well as his role in the *American Pie* trilogy, so it was pretty cool to get to meet him. We had a great time talking about our goals and the projects we had or were working on. But I think all of us knew that what started as a couple of people having fun would eventually turn into a really great business partnership. And a few months later, I ended up helping Tim and Thom promote and distribute their film.

I was able to do all of these exciting things and meet all of these wonderful people simply because I opened myself up to the opportunity to have a great time. All work should start out and ultimately stay fun, just as all work partners should start out as and ultimately stay friends. To me, that's the only way to succeed when doing anything in life.

PRODUCTION ASSISTANT'S TASKS

☆ Learn to look at obstacles as opportunities.
Getting frustrated is a waste of time and will derail
your life script.

☆ Use your imagination to work on your dream.
If you come up with an idea that someone else has
already patented, brainstorm new ideas. Keep pushing
yourself—don't give up on your dream just because
someone else has the same one. You can tailor your
dream and edit your life script as you go along.

☆ Think about how your dream can help other
people.
What problem are you solving? What service are you
providing?

☆ Make sure, first and foremost, that you are
having fun as you move toward your goal.
The more fun you have, the more you will attract
attention from others that may help you get closer to
what you want.

CHAPTER 4

The Pitch:
Turn a No into a Go

Y ou know that to reach any dream, you have to take action. Part of taking action involves working with other people. Now that you've written and edited your life script and reminded yourself that this process of reaching your dream is all about fun, you have to put your script out in the world and try to get others to buy into it. It's time to pitch your script. And once you start pitching, no matter what your dream is, there's always a chance that someone will tell you no. In fact, it's almost certain that someone will.

Don't Take No for an Answer

There are a million reasons why someone might tell you no. Some people may say no because they can't help you. Others may say no because they don't believe in you. Still others may be too busy, too threatened by you, or too afraid that your dream will somehow negatively impact their own (if you're pitching a movie to a filmmaker working on a similar movie, you can bet he won't jump to help you out).

> CHRIS: When people tell you no, they usually don't beat around the bush: "That's ridiculous." "That will never work." "Are you insane?" But no matter what someone says, it doesn't mean you can't accomplish what you set out to do.

Whatever the reason behind a no, even if it seems valid at first, it may be wrong. Here is an example. Back in the 1970s, a young director made a movie that became one of the most profitable films of all time. Fresh from this success, he wrote a script and offered it to various studios—and they all turned him down. Universal Studios even dismissed this director's script as "unfathomable" and "silly." To the director's delight, Twentieth Century Fox decided to take a chance and greenlight the project. It could see the film's unique potential. However, during production, the film went over budget, and the studio came close to canceling it altogether. In desperation, the director showed his partially completed film to studio executives, but since he hadn't completed the ending, he substituted old black-and-white footage from World War II to give the studio executives an idea of how the movie would end. Needless to say, the studio executives were not impressed.

As a last resort, the director offered to keep the film alive by supporting it with his own money. In return for paying the production costs, the director negotiated to retain the rights to all future sequels, along with merchandising rights for the characters in the film. At the time, merchandising rights were considered nearly worthless, so the studio agreed. The director financed the rest of the film out of his own pocket, and on May 25, 1977, released it to theaters under the name *Star Wars.*

The lesson here is obvious: don't ever take no for an answer. By following this advice, George Lucas succeeded beyond his wildest dreams.

 DIRECTOR'S NOTES: Never accept no, regardless of who says it and why.

One Yes Is More Important Than a Million Nos

The only person you absolutely must get to say yes to your dreams is you. Yours is the only yes that matters. If you tell yourself that you're allowed to pursue your dreams every day, then no one can kill your plans instantaneously. So it is imperative that you give yourself the go-ahead.

You may hear nos from your friends, your family members, or your coworkers. You may hear them from potential employers, teachers, guidance counselors, bank loan managers, film festival or literary journal judges, coaches, or admissions boards. You might hear a no for reasons that have nothing to do with your talent, skills, or abilities. In some cases, the person may just be telling you no for the moment or for a specific project or opportunity. Hollywood casting directors routinely dismiss actors because they need someone who looks like they could be the son or daughter of a major movie star. If you don't fit that description, the casting director can't use you, no matter how talented you may be.

> EFREN: I once auditioned for a part in a movie that I was really excited about. I wanted the role and thought that I could do a great job playing the character. I was fully prepared, and I nailed the audition. Unfortunately, I didn't get the role. I was disappointed. I even began to doubt myself. But it's not about how hard you fall, it's about how hard you punch. You get up and you move forward. Every audition, every interview, I show them who I am, I show them what I can do, and I own the room.

The trick to dealing with all these nos is to realize that every successful person has run into the same wall of discouragement. Don't take rejection personally.

As long as you can say yes to your dreams, a million people can tell you no, and you'll still have the only person in your corner you'll need to pursue your dream.

 DIRECTOR'S NOTES: The only person who can kill your dreams by saying no is you.

The Importance of Hearing a No

Nobody likes to hear no, but it can actually help you find a way to get someone to tell you yes. For example, suppose you wanted to design your own jewelry and open your own store.

BEHIND THE SCENES: Ken Davitian

The last person you want to tell you no is someone whom you admire and respect. However, even that can't stop you if you don't let it, which is exactly what happened to a friend of ours, actor Ken Davitian, who played Azamat Bagatov in *Borat: Cultural Learnings of America for Make Benefit Glorious Nation of Kazakhstan*. Here's his story.

I was 17 years old and the lead actor in all of my high school plays at Garfield High School in East Los Angeles. I knew way before then that I wanted to be an actor. Our drama department was hosting a guest speaker, and I was in charge of making sure that everything went well for our guest. After all these years, his name escapes me, but I remember distinctly that he was a famous Latino star for the series *High Chaparral*.

He saw me perform an opening skit on stage for his speaking engagement. At the end, when I was walking him out of the auditorium, I told him, "I want to be an actor and be on a television series just like you!"

That's when he turned over his right shoulder, looked me in the eye, and said, "You'll never be an actor," and then he walked away. It was the most discouraging and devastating moment in my adolescence. However at that moment, I realized I would never take no for an answer.

For the past 30 years, I have worked to prove him wrong by continually honing my craft and never giving

(continued)

up. I have struggled at times but persevered by remembering what he said to me. And now as I look back, I realize that he helped me more than he hurt me. If you believe in yourself and if you've done everything mentally, physically, and spiritually possible to achieve your goal, then you've already succeeded. ★

You apply for a loan from the bank, and you are told that it can't offer you one. Instead of slinking away in defeat, ask for the reason why. By listening to the loan officer, you can better understand what part of your plan you might need to fix. Perhaps you didn't prove your ability to pay back the loan, or perhaps your mission statement isn't clear enough. With this information in hand, you can patch up these problems and try again.

Hearing nos can even steer you in a better direction. If you hear enough of them, you might find it's time to try a different approach. Even though your heart is set on opening your own jewelry store, if you are unable to get a loan, it might be time to get creative and start an Internet-based jewelry business out of your own home or try to sell your jewelry to existing jewelry stores. After a while, you might make enough money to convince someone to grant you a loan. Just because someone says no today doesn't mean that she will say no tomorrow, especially if you've changed in the meantime.

 DIRECTOR'S NOTES: Don't take no as a rejection; take it as a challenge.

Dealing with Criticism

In the words of famed Hollywood screenwriter William Gold-man, "Nobody knows anything." That means everyone may have a reason to criticize your dreams, but that doesn't mean that everyone is right. Look at how many studio executives turned down *Star Wars* in 1977 because they didn't think anyone would want to see a science fiction movie about some guy named Luke Skywalker. Now consider that in that same year, studio executives were rushing to green-light the movie *Exorcist II: The Heretic,* which completely bombed in the box office. So the next time someone tells you no, it doesn't automatically mean that he's right. In fact, there's a good chance that anyone telling you no is dead wrong.

But the fact that someone is wrong doesn't make criticism any easier to hear. The only way to withstand criticism is to believe in yourself and not take the criticism as a personal attack. Protect your dream from others' negativity. The reason so many people fail to achieve their dreams isn't because they can't achieve them but because they fail to protect their dreams from being derailed by critics. And sometimes the biggest critic you have to overcome is yourself.

CHRIS: Handling criticism is a lot like reading minds, and you might be surprised to discover that you can learn to do both. When people say no, their character and their circumstances can reveal the source of their negativity. Their no might mean "I'm jealous I didn't think of that idea first" or "I don't believe that extraordinary

BEHIND THE SCENES: Ari Gold

Our colleague Ari Gold (a young film director, not the character from *Entourage*) won a student Academy Award in 2000 for his film *Helicopter*, and his *The Adventures of Power* premiered at the 2008 Sundance Film Festival. Here is his account of fighting through the nos.

I can't count the number of times people have told me no, but I will say that the projects I've completed (three short films and a feature) all had this in common: I loved them enough to ignore the no and fight to find a yes, even if it had to come from elsewhere. If you accept the no, you might not love what you're doing enough. ★

things are possible because I haven't found them for myself." Being able to interpret a no means being able to overcome it.

If anyone, including you, questions or criticizes your dream, you need to focus your life on achieving your dream so that nothing can shake your foundation. For example, suppose your dream is to finish the Boston Marathon. Everyone around you doubts that you can do it, saying you're too old or too young or that you've never done it before. This type of (really mean) criticism could hurt your feelings—but only if you doubt yourself.

EFREN: Even when I was told that I wasn't an actor,
I knew in my heart that I was. And I would never
let anyone stop me.

The only thing you can do is prepare for the run and commit to doing your best. Even your harshest critics won't be able to criticize the fact that you wake up at five o'clock every morning and run ten miles before work.

 DIRECTOR'S NOTES: Don't focus on the criticism; focus on reaching your dreams.

Saying Yes to Yourself Pays Off in the End

Success is no accident. You have to work hard to turn your dream into reality, despite the nos and the criticism. Just as you have to tell yourself yes, you have to keep actively pursuing your goal no matter what. If you don't, you'll end up taking whatever comes your way. That's no fun.

Let's look at a remarkable story of someone who kept going despite the risk involved. In the 1970s, a young man from Seattle whose father was a prominent lawyer with his own law firm enrolled at Harvard as a prelaw major. With his SAT score, this man could have coasted through Harvard, attended law school, and gotten a job at his father's law firm. That would have been easy, and it would have made him a wealthy man as well. But he had other ideas.

Instead of pursuing a law degree, he dropped out of Harvard because he found mathematics more interesting than law. Instead of moving back in with his parents, he moved to Albuquerque after reading a magazine story about a New Mexico company that had developed the world's first personal computer. He offered to sell a computer program he had written to this company, and it agreed to buy it. The only problem? He hadn't written the program yet. How's that for an obstacle?

But rather than panic, the man spent the next few weeks writing the program he had promised, day and night. When he demonstrated it to the computer company, it liked what it saw and agreed to buy it. Although the computer company soon went out of business, this young man, who gave up a more predictable life as a lawyer and took the much harder route of starting his own software company, stayed in business. He called his company Micro-soft (later changed to Microsoft). This daring young man was none other than Bill Gates.

CHRIS: When I was looking at colleges, I could have taken the easy way out and gone to a local state university, even though my dream was to attend Pepperdine University in California. If I hadn't dared to try for my dream, I wouldn't be where I am today.

Gates succeeded because he dared to pursue his passion and wound up creating an empire. If he had pursued law just because it was easy and not because it was something he wanted to do, he could have done well for himself, but he wouldn't have been nearly as successful. That's why it's important for you to find your passion in life and pursue it until you succeed.

It's okay to feel discouraged at times. If criticism and obstacles have dampened your enthusiasm, just do the smallest, easiest task in your life script. This could mean researching schools, brushing up your darkroom skills, polishing your resume, or going for a jog. The trick is to keep moving forward, no matter how insignificant your progress may seem. Over time, even the tiniest steps forward can translate into massive leaps of progress.

 DIRECTOR'S NOTES: The only way you can fail is to quit. Over time, even the tiniest steps forward can translate into leaps of progress.

HOW I HANDLED DOUBT

Efren

While pursuing my dream, I often felt like a pirate in search of treasure, sailing the open seas. Inevitably, if you sail long enough, you're going to run into storms that can divert you from your course. By surviving each storm, you can test your determination and resolve.

I ran into a "perfect storm" in college. I was taking a drama course, studying a scene written by John Patrick Shandley in the play *Danny and the Deep Blue Sea*. I had thrown myself into rehearsals and was excited to perform the scene with my partner on stage. After my performance, I turned to my drama teacher for what I hoped would be recognition of my abilities and encouragement to keep pursuing my dream. I got neither.

Instead, my teacher told me I was like lightning—full of energy but too raw. Though a lovely metaphor, his criticism was not constructive. I didn't think I could feel any worse until he opened up the criticism to the rest of the class. Some said I was all over the place; others said I was too chaotic. Some even said that I wasn't right for the role.

I left the class that day with my head hung low. I remember walking back to my car, sitting down, and asking myself what really mattered to me. I asked myself why I was in an acting class and why I was even bothering to go to school. That's when I decided that I had a choice: I could ignore what was said, or I could ignore what I wanted to do. I knew I couldn't ignore my passion, so I vowed to take the class's criticism as a chance to get better at my craft.

I knew I had to get better. I needed to learn, and to learn, I needed the right books. For actors in Los Angeles, the right books are in the Samuel French bookstore, and that's when I made that bookstore my second home. For the next few months, I read everything I could get my hands on about acting. Reading all those books opened my eyes to a world of acting that I'd never before known existed. I learned that acting had several different branches and schools of thought and that no one branch or school of thought was necessarily better or worse than the others. That's when I realized that I could learn different techniques and styles.

But I needed to buy those books that held the key to unlocking the acting world I dreamed about. That's when my real passion for acting took off. I got a job to pay for my books, and I spent the rest of my time studying the craft. Some of my old friends didn't understand my dream. So I spent much of my time alone. But that was all right, because I knew that following my dream was the only way I could truly be happy.

THE ONLY YES I NEEDED
Chris

The first time I thought about taking a no at face value was my last. When I was a teenager, I spent a fortune on concert tickets. I've always loved music, but trying to see all of my favorite bands when they came to town got to be a pretty pricey habit. I started wondering if there was a way to go to all the concerts I wanted to attend without spending all of my money. When I started to brainstorm about how to get into concerts for free, my friends told me it couldn't be done. I didn't hear anyone say yes.

A kid from my town who was a couple of years older than me started his own business of setting up local concerts. He was able to bring nationally known artists to our relatively small town, all because he knew how to get the word out to kids in the area and generate good money through ticket sales. I saw this guy putting on huge shows at an age when most people made minimum wage at fast-food joints or retail stores. Best of all, he got to hang out with artists most kids dreamed about just seeing in concert.

I knew I had a lot in common with this guy because I loved music just as much as he did. Seeing him put on shows was enough of a yes to motivate me to do what I wanted to do in the music world. So I came up with an idea that would help me get into concerts for free and bring publicity to my favorite bands and the people who were staging their shows: I decided to be a music journalist. I figured that bands want ticket sales, and more people buy tickets when they know about a really great show. So I started my own music website and began writing reviews of all of the concerts I'd seen. I found out that people are eager to get firsthand opinions about shows, so my site started receiving a lot of hits. Once I got a lot of attention, I started showing up at band managers' doors and offering to write reviews of their bands in exchange for concert tickets. The band managers loved the idea of getting extra exposure for their bands by giving out concert tickets. My idea worked! I got to see all the shows I wanted for free by writing reviews of the bands on my site. I even got to interview some of them, like Reel Big Fish, Weezer, and Green Day.

After finding success with my music journalism career, I wanted to share my secrets with other kids my age. I wanted to be able to give others a big yes to their dreams where I had only received a lot of nos. I started thinking about what would have helped me get started writing concert reviews. I came up with the idea of writing and selling a guidebook about how to get into concerts for free.

Of course, I got a bunch of nos to my new idea; a lot of my friends responded by saying, "Who would want to spend money on something like that?" But my friends hadn't been right the first time, so I didn't give their nos a second thought. I knew that what I wanted to write for other people was exactly what I would have loved to have had for myself; if I would spend my money on it, I believed that other people would, too.

So I spent my summer vacation that year writing, publishing, and printing my guidebook. I made a website that would correspond with and provide information on my product. I discovered the beauty of eBay, where I could market the book to thousands of kids all across the country who wanted to buy it. Pretty soon, I was receiving thousands of orders and, over time, I made over $100,000 on a book that people had told me "no one would ever want." The only way I was able to do it was to view the nos as just negative talk. I gave myself the yes I needed.

PRODUCTION ASSISTANT'S TASKS

☆ Pitch your life script to yourself.
Your yes is the most important one.

☆ Listen to criticism but don't assume it's right.
When people criticize you, take in what they are saying only if it helps to get you closer to your dream.

☆ Take risks.
Taking the easy way out will not bring you to the heights of success.

ACT II

PRODUCTION: MAKE A PLAN
AND BUILD YOUR TEAM

CHAPTER 5

Make Your Plans (and Your Budget) for Success

Now that someone has given you a yes for your script — that's right, you — it's time to start planning your dream in more detail. To make a movie shoot happen, a filmmaker must develop a shooting plan and a budget. These tasks may seem overwhelming, but if you start small, everything will get done, and soon you'll be smack in the middle of the dream that you created.

Start Local

Every day, hundreds of Hollywood hopefuls move to Los Angeles to achieve their dream of breaking into show business. But just because someone lives in the greater metropolitan Los Angeles area doesn't mean their dream will automatically come true. If she has no skills or experience in show business before she moves to L.A., she'll still have no skills or experience in show business when she gets to L.A. Even worse, she'll be competing against people who do have connections, skills, and experience in show business, which makes the odds of success in the field even lower.

It's true that you need a plan to get your dream going, and that plan can include a move to a city that supports what you want to do—like a move to New York if you want to work in publishing or on Wall Street, or a move to Washington, D.C., because you want to break into politics. But smart people don't move somewhere and expect the place itself to make their dreams come true. Smart people start pursuing their dreams right where they are. If you want to become an actor, start taking acting classes and looking for theater auditions in your hometown. If you don't have the dedication and persistence to learn how to act and audition for roles where you live now, you probably won't have the dedication or persistence in Los Angeles, either.

CHRIS: Consider writer Elizabeth Licorish. Elizabeth seized every opportunity to get her writing out into the world, from writing movie, music, and book reviews to political editorials, short essays, and book proposals. Eventually, her work was seen by one of the world's greatest scientists, David Pensak, and the two decided to form a team in writing a book intended to change the way the world thinks about innovation.

Aspiring singers can join a choir; future baseball players can join a team in their town or at their school. So instead of making plans to move, step one of your plan should be to think about what you can do right now to turn your life script into a reality. If you start local, you'll lay the foundation to go anywhere in the world.

 DIRECTOR'S NOTES: You can take the first step toward your dream right now, no matter where you are.

Start Small

Suppose you want to become a film director. If you've never directed a film before, what are the odds that you'd succeed if Universal Studios suddenly gave you the green light and $70 million? No matter how many resources or how much money you had, chances are you'd make a critical mistake and wind up failing to make the movie.

However, you *can* make a movie if you start small. A 3-minute short film is much easier to make than a 120-minute movie. Grab a camcorder, film a 3-minute skit that you wrote, using yourself as the "star," and post it on YouTube. *Voilà!*—you've made a movie. The more short films you make, the more you'll learn about filmmaking. Eventually, you'll gain the confidence and abilities to be able to tackle larger, more challenging projects. Every small success is a step in the right direction. If you try to tackle too large a project, you could get overwhelmed and fail, but if you tackle that same project after several years of finishing smaller ones, that larger project will be much easier for you to complete and succeed.

In addition to giving you a bit of confidence and a sense of achievement, starting small provides a safe arena in which to make mistakes. If you want to become a stand-up comedian, you don't want your first time on stage to be on *The Tonight Show* in front of millions of people on national television. Bombing on *The Tonight Show* could end your career before it gets started. A better alternative would be to perform at an open-mic night at your local comedy club or coffeehouse. Then you can make your mistakes — because everyone makes them when they're starting out — in front of a small, forgiving crowd.

Try setting some small goals for yourself. Small goals are always easier to reach than big ones, and once you succeed at a smaller goal, you'll have the motivation to tackle much larger ones.

 DIRECTOR'S NOTES: Every small success is a step in the right direction.

Forget about "Overnight" Success

There are no shortcuts to success. If you decide you want to become a tennis star, you could buy the most expensive tennis racket, a whole wardrobe of whites, and hire the best coaches, but if you don't take the time to develop your talent and skills, you'll likely fail.

Consider Angelina Jolie. Despite being the daughter of Academy Award–winning actor Jon Voight, she spent most of her early acting career appearing in her brother's student films at the University of Southern California. Rather than using her famous father to get ahead, she continued learning

BEHIND THE SCENES: Jay Galvin

Jay Galvin runs his own business called Private Concierge, which caters to financial executives. When Wall Street types want to reward their top earners by taking them to Las Vegas for a weekend, they call Jay. His company makes travel itineraries, including flights, hotel accommodations, restaurants, nightlife venues, shows, and concerts. But Private Concierge wasn't Jay's first business.

My parents used to take me to the beach in the summer every year while I was growing up. It was during those summers that I had my very first business experience. On the way to the beach each day, my mother would stop by the grocery store to pick up drinks and food. Outside of the grocery store, there were vending machines filled with different types of toys that cost a quarter. I would beg my mother for a few dollars worth of quarters and buy as many toys as I possibly could. Once we got to the beach, I would spread out a towel and lay the toys on top to sell to people walking by. I sold each toy for $0.50, creating a 100 percent profit.

Another of my businesses started when I was about 13 years old in the winter. When it snowed, I would round up my friends and create three teams with three people per team. Then we'd head out and go door-to-door, asking if anyone would like us to shovel their walkway, driveway, sidewalk, or path to

(continued)

their garbage. The leaders of the group, whom I had appointed, charged each house $45, tip included. On a good day, each group ended up doing six houses. We earned $90 each for a little over three hours of work.

Even though these were seasonal occupations, for me they were stepping stones to entrepreneurship. They were small tasks, but it was better than not starting at all. It helped me learn about dialogue, selling my services, and building relationships. Once you realize that you have the power to create your goals and determine the right steps in achieving them, you can succeed at anything you set your mind to do. ★

her craft through small roles in low-budget films (remember *Cyborg 2?*) and music videos. Over time, she landed roles in higher-profile films, such as *Hackers* and *Girl, Interrupted.* Today, as we all know, Jolie is herself an Academy Award–winning actor and international movie star. But she didn't get there overnight. She started small, gained confidence, and worked her way up to bigger and meatier roles. You can follow in her footsteps to achieve your dreams.

And as Efren tells you throughout the book, he started in his neighborhood and on small stages before ending up on the silver screen.

"Overnight" success only happens after years of hard work that the public never sees, as we both know. When someone becomes an "overnight" success, look into his background, and you'll find that in most cases, the media ignored him for years as he struggled to achieve the dream. You don't need money or connections to succeed. You only need the determination to start where you are, gain small successes, and turn your experiences into stepping stones for much larger successes, until you become the next "overnight" success in your own chosen career.

 DIRECTOR'S NOTES: "Overnight" success only happens after years of hard work.

Just Start!

Okay, now it's time to think about your budget. Almost everyone has heard that it takes money to make money, but we're here to tell you that that's wrong. It doesn't take money to make money. It takes ideas to make money.

When you're starting out, you'll probably need money. You may need it to pay for classes, books, or equipment and will need it for the basics like food, shelter, and clothing. Although many people believe that they could get started if they only had enough money, the opposite is true. Too much money can actually be a hindrance. For example, suppose you wanted to open your own restaurant. If you had a lot of money to spend, you might be tempted to lease a huge space, decorate it with expensive lighting and furniture, and buy the best kitchen appliances you could find. With such massive financial resources, you might think that the restaurant's success is guaranteed, but it isn't. If you concentrate on the things in your restaurant, and not your vision of it, you may overlook crucial elements of the business, such as what your customers really want to eat. Consider the alternative. Instead of wasting thousands of dollars creating a fancy-looking restaurant, if you start small, you'll be able to test the market and change to meet its demands.

> EFREN: Never let lack of money be an excuse for why you can't pursue your dreams. The less money you have, the more creative and dedicated you'll need to be, and that means a greater chance of success in the future.

Don't look at a lack of financial resources as a handicap but as a blessing. If you have a lot of money, you might be tempted to pay consultants, advertising agencies, and marketing firms to promote your restaurant. Chances are, they'll charge you a lot, and if their marketing and advertising campaigns work, you'll be stuck relying on someone else to do it for you again. If their marketing and advertising campaigns don't work, you won't have a clue why they didn't, and you won't know how to fix or change them without paying someone else to figure it out. But if you start with as little money as possible, you'll be forced to do all your marketing and advertising yourself, and you'll quickly learn what works and what doesn't at little cost. Once you know what works for your business, you'll have this knowledge forever and can apply it to your next business venture.

DIRECTOR'S NOTES: Lack of money can never stop you from achieving your dreams.

Make Your Own Money

Always look at money as a tool to get you where you want to be, not as your ultimate goal. While some dreams do have the potential of making you a multimillionaire, such as becoming an inventor or starting your own Internet company, others, such as working to save orphans in Somalia or building your own house, have little or no chance of making you rich. So let's talk about how you can make enough money to get you started.

Obviously, the simplest way to make money is to get a job. A lot of struggling actors, musicians, and artists support themselves by working "day jobs" as waiters, retail store clerks, proofreaders, or dog-walkers (the list could go on) while they pursue their dreams. All you need is enough money to survive and a job that is flexible enough to allow you time to work on your goal. The biggest challenge is that you remain focused on your dream while you earn a living. But if you are truly passionate about what you are striving for, that won't be too much of a problem.

Dedication to your passion can literally take you from nothing to everything. Here's a story of someone who experienced exactly that. A divorced woman with a one-year-old baby found herself unemployed and living off welfare in Edinburgh, Scotland. After being diagnosed with clinical depression, this woman spent her time writing a novel in nearby cafés. After completing her novel, she submitted it to 12 different publishers, which all rejected it. A publisher finally agreed to publish her book because the editor's eight-year-old daughter had read the first chapter and demanded the rest. Despite his daughter's enthusiasm, the editor warned the author, J. K. Rowling, to get a day job because it was unlikely that she would ever make money with a children's book called *Harry Potter and the Philosopher's Stone* (renamed in the United States as *Harry Potter and the Sorcerer's Stone*). You know the rest of the story.

J. K. Rowling's story demonstrates that you can achieve your dream by starting with hardly any money at all and that if you create something worthwhile, you may not have to get a day job (although this is pretty rare). Whether you have a day job or not, keep in mind that the true purpose of money is to help you continue doing what you love.

 DIRECTOR'S NOTES: Money is important, but it's never the goal in itself.

Spend Your Own Money

Since you're the first person who said yes to your dream, you'll likely be the first person who will invest in your dream, as well. While it may be tempting to ask to borrow money from others such as friends or relatives, spend your own money first.

Ultimately, the more money you get from others, the more restrictions you'll place on your dream. Borrowing money from family members can be somewhat restrictive, but borrowing money from banks or other financial institutions can be even worse. Navigating through the bureaucracy and paperwork to get a loan from a bank or financial institution can be cumbersome, and most banks prefer lending money to established businesses that they understand. Back in 1977, no bank wanted to loan money to two guys who wanted to build and sell personal computers. Hardly anyone in these banks had even heard of a personal computer, let alone thought about buying one, so for a bank to turn down a loan request from a personal computer company made perfect sense. But Steve Jobs and Steve Wozniak didn't give up. They managed to fund their fledgling computer company with their own money, even selling an old Volkswagen bus for cash. As the company grew and personal computers became more popular, banks began to realize that loaning money to Apple Computers was no longer a risk but a smart business decision.

When you're first getting started, start small, use your own cash, and if you must borrow money from friends or family, borrow as little as possible. Once you become a success, your chances of getting a traditional bank loan become much higher. Don't necessarily ignore banks and other lending institutions when you're getting started, but don't count on them, either. After all, no bank will have as much faith in your dream as you will.

EFREN: Money is a responsibility. Before you bring in financial partners, you must be clear on how to manage what you have invested, whether it's a dollar, a grand, or a million. So many put

themselves in debt because they lose sight of
their life's responsibilities. You can't go out and
spend money before taking care of the necessi-
ties in your life.

If you spend your own money, you're much more likely
to spend wisely and buy only the items that you absolutely
need, like art supplies if you want to become a cartoonist
or basic cookware and kitchen tools if you want to become
a chef. You'll also place a higher value on these items than
if someone bought them for you, since you're the one who
worked to earn enough money to buy them. In turn, you'll
probably use them more and achieve much more as a result.
More importantly, spending your own money verifies your
own commitment to your dream. If you aren't willing to work
and contribute monetarily to achieve your dream, you probably don't want your dream badly enough.

Consider the determination and sacrifice of one of the
most famous and successful people in the world. An aspiring
dancer decided to leave the comfort of a dance scholarship
at the University of Michigan and move to New York City
with $35 to her name to pursue a dance career. Although her
father was an engineer at General Motors and could have
supported her financially, she took a series of minimum wage
jobs to support herself. Soon, she began writing and singing
her own dance songs, which attracted the attention of a record
producer at Sire Records. After her first two singles became
minor hits on the dance charts, Sire decided that this young
singer needed to release a complete album, which it decided

to name after the singer herself: *Madonna*. Madonna's debut album spawned three hit singles, and this former dancer soon found her greatest success dancing to her own songs as one of the best-selling female vocalists in the world.

Perhaps Madonna could have succeeded just as well if her father had paid for her to move to New York and sent her an allowance so she could concentrate on her dance career. However, she chose to rely on herself. If you rely on money from others, you may never truly feel committed to your dreams. The moment you start relying on yourself, you'll have already achieved a level of success that nobody can ever take away from you.

☆ **DIRECTOR'S NOTES:** Spending your own money shows your own commitment to your dream.
If you aren't willing to work or pay to achieve your dream, you probably don't want your dream badly enough.

Ask for Other People's Money

Sometimes it's impossible to pay for your dream all by yourself. For example, hardly anyone has enough money to open a clothing store or pay for the fuel needed to fly a private airplane around the world. If your dream is bigger than your wallet, the next best thing is to borrow money from people whose wallets are fatter than yours. Sometimes this means asking relatives for a loan.

To convince people in your family to give or loan you money, you'll need to convince them that your dream is important, that you're serious about pursuing it, and that you'll do your utmost to succeed. In other words, you need to pitch them your idea. Remember, if you can't convince others that you'll achieve your dream, you probably haven't convinced yourself that you can. If they are convinced and agree to help you, make sure everyone knows exactly what's expected. Some relatives may give you money outright with no questions asked. Others may expect you to pay back the money at a certain time, with or without interest. Most will want to see the progress you are making with their investment. Be sure to keep your family apprised of the progress you make and be sure to thank them at every opportunity. For example, Efren's family was very supportive of his education, helping him out financially. He shared his joys and challenges with his family, and no one could have been happier when his acting career took off.

Chris knows a lot about raising money, since he has done it on a number of occasions. He offers the following suggestions:

- If you're using the money to start a business, money from relatives may represent partial ownership of your business, so let all your funders know how much control they'll have over the way the business is run. As you can see, the more you rely on money from others, the less freedom you'll have to do what you want, and the more people you'll need to answer to. That's okay, because if the business prospers,

BEHIND THE SCENES: Sean Covel

Sean Covel, one of the young producers of *Napoleon Dynamite*, was in a unique situation as he tried to find funding for the movie. After falling in love with the quirky script, Sean and the other producers knew the movie would be a risky investment. They wrote the smallest budget they knew they could make the film with—about $400,000. To make the movie into something that would attract investors, the producers made the *Napoleon* project just one part of a three-part slate, meaning that it would be part of a trio of low-budget projects, each in a different genre and made by different filmmakers. But *Napoleon Dynamite* surpassed even Sean's highest expectations, becoming one of the most beloved and best-selling movie hits of the decade.

I had to be really honest with investors up front. I told them, "Listen, if people get the jokes in *Napoleon*, the picture could blow up and do unbelievably great business. But if people don't get the jokes, your money will go away completely and forever." But since the other movies in the slate would be horror movies—guaranteeing cable, DVD, and foreign sales even if they didn't get theatrical release—then if *Napoleon* bombed, at least the other two films would make up for the loss. An important part of securing investors for a film or any other creative project is to assure them that they are not putting all their eggs in one basket.

(continued)

The movie was such a success because it was given the freedom by its producers and investors to be quirky, different, and against the mainstream. The best way to attract the attention of investors, clients, and fans is to be specific in what you are trying to achieve. The reason *Napoleon Dynamite* was such a triumphant independent film was because it told such a unique story about specific people in a specific place—things that huge movie studios aren't trying to do with their films because their aim is to make a ton of money by appealing to a general audience. When you are starting out on your own and taking on well-established people and businesses, the trick is to do something different; if you try to do the same things as the big guys, you won't be able to win.

When putting together a proposal for investors, include the specifics of the project, such as: exactly how many dollars are needed from start to finish, a time line of how the money will be spent across the major events of the project, an outline of how the recoup of the investment will work and how the profits will be split amongst the investors, what credit the investors will receive, and case studies of how investment deals worked in similar projects. And don't forget to pay yourself. Investors will expect you to do this, because if you are living out of a box, you probably won't be able to work hard enough to make your project a success. But paying yourself

(continued)

doesn't mean blowing 90 percent of your budget on your personal expenses. It means allotting yourself enough for the basics like food and rent, enough for you to be able to get the job done. ★

you can always pay back your relatives with interest and buy back their shares of the business. (Just make sure your relatives agree that you can buy them out under certain conditions.)

- If you can't or don't want to approach family members for money, start looking around. There are successful doctors, lawyers, businesspeople, and sports stars in almost every town. Most people are willing to take risks with their money, *if* they believe in you—so make sure you have your pitch down. Start networking online and at events in your town or city. A really important thing you can do for yourself is to create business cards. By printing your dream job title beneath your name on a business card, you are solidifying your dream in your own mind and creating a professional image of yourself for others to see. Anyone can make a business card, and once you do, you will be pleasantly surprised at how well people will respond to what you are trying to accomplish.

- By going after an investment from an individual and not a loan from a bank, you aren't just asking for cash; you are asking for other people's faith in what you want to do. So while getting an investor is a lot more difficult than borrowing on credit, it ultimately means that your projects will be a lot safer. Obviously, you won't be held to deadlines and interest rates when it comes to paying the money back. But the real reason it pays to look for investors is that pitching your endeavor will really motivate you to make sure it is as solid as possible.

- Still can't find anyone to invest in your project? Look online. Today, a new way to finance just about any dream you have is peer-to-peer lending. One company at the forefront of this innovation is called LendingClub.com. Instead of maxing out a credit card to start a new business, you can take out a loan from a group of people at a lower interest rate than you would pay to a credit card company or bank. All you need to do is post your loan request on the site so that potential investors can get an idea of what your project is. This arrangement is a win-win for investors and borrowers, because investors split up the investment so that any losses they may suffer will be small, which in turn causes the borrower's interest rates to be small as well. For example, right now on LendingClub.com, a member needs $25,000 to start a DVD vending machine rental company. He has already had $24,300 invested, so he only needs $700 more before his loan is filled and he will be able to launch his company.

 DIRECTOR'S NOTES: There is money out there; you just have to know how to find it.

IT'S NOT ALWAYS EASY, BUT IT'S ALWAYS WORTH IT

Efren

Speaking strictly from an artist's point of view, the letters *a-r-t* are nowhere to be found in the word *money*. If you are pursuing big money through the arts, good luck. Although both can be passions, you must ask yourself what means the most to you and be clear about what you need and what you want.

However or wherever you are in your financial situation, accept where you are and take it from there. If you need a job, so be it. If you need two, so be that. When I was starting out as an actor, I had many jobs to support myself. I had to pay for rent, school tuition, bus fare, and books. Although I held so many different jobs, I always kept my bigger goal in mind. Some jobs paid more than others, and some jobs didn't pay at all, like the student films I worked in just for the experience. Some jobs even cost me money to do them, like performing in theater productions that only drew five audience members per show. But I needed that experience, too, so I forgot about the fact that I wasn't going to get paid and focused on the fact that I could add the role to my acting resume. I wanted my dream of making it as a professional actor badly enough to be willing to pay the price to get there.

HOW I FINANCED *AFTER SCHOOL*
Chris

Even before the ink was dry on my contract with First USA, I knew I was in for some major financial training.

First USA taught me a lot about the finer points of finance, but the most important thing I learned is really the simplest concept: don't spend more money than you have. So if you already owe a ton of money to credit card companies and banks, I suggest you put this book down for a bit and read another one about how to eliminate personal debt. Just like directing a movie, directing your own life takes a reasonable amount of money, and you probably won't be able to do it if you're saddled with debt.

The reality is that you might have to borrow more money yourself to accomplish your dream. If the director of any one of today's biggest box office hits had to finance the project himself, hardly any of the world's greatest movies would have ever been made. There's nothing wrong with borrowing money to invest in a project. If you work hard and succeed, you will be able to pay the money back. But don't approach potential investors until you have a solid plan to sell to them. When I started planning my first documentary, *After School*, I only had a little money—just enough to start a website. I developed the film's concept and mission over the Internet. Once I came up with a solid vision for my project, I had something real to show investors so that the money they lent me had a clear place to go.

I needed to raise some serious cash. I needed funds for travel, film equipment, crew, and even food. Even though Kevin Smith had been a huge inspiration to me in the way he gave everything he had (including his entire credit limit) to his films, I didn't want to follow the exact model of how he got his first movie made, because credit card companies still want their money back even if a movie flops. So I decided to find investors. By doing this, I found out that sometimes it is useful to try to convince your investors to finance just a small part of your project at a time. When it came to funding *After School,* our first investor wanted to see what we could produce, so he put in only enough money to get us started. Then when we showed him some amazing footage, he was ready to cut a check big enough to get the film made.

PRODUCTION ASSISTANT'S TASKS

☆ Start working on your dream today, wherever you live.

Sign up for a class, talk to someone in the field you wish to pursue, sing in the shower—whatever step you take will get you one step closer to success.

☆ Make a plan.

Start with the simplest things you can do today to start moving forward. Think small and specific.

☆ Squash your dreams of becoming an overnight success.

Only years of hard work and dedication will get you where you want to be. Stay focused on progress, not the end result.

☆ Don't let lack of money stop you.

A lot of people started from nothing and became very successful; you can, too.

☆ Make a budget.

Figure out how much you'll need to make to support your basic needs, then how much you'll need to support the first steps of your dream.

☆ Work to earn money.

Use this money as your first drop in the bucket instead of relying on other people's money.

☆ If you must, perfect your pitch and get
others to invest in your dream.
Make business cards, start a website, go to local events
where you'll meet people who could help you. You'll
never get anyone to invest in your dream unless you
convince them to do so.

CHAPTER 6

Assemble Your
Cast and Crew

Obviously, an integral part of every film is a cast and crew. Surrounding yourself with the right people is a necessary part of achieving anything. The support of people like teachers, mentors, colleagues, and friends is a crucial component in developing your dream. In addition to providing support, the people around you will be able to teach you new things.

There are two ways to learn anything. You can fumble around on your own, learning through trial and error, and banging your head and bruising your shins as you stumble your way toward success. Or you can find someone to teach you what you need to know. By learning from others, you can shorten the path to any goal.

CHRIS: Whenever I am launching a new project, I always try to determine who I know that can help me turn it into a success. If I don't know anyone, it's time to look outside my contact list.

Learn from the Experts

To learn from anyone, you must first know what you want. Once you've defined your dream and visualized exactly what you want and where you want to be, you can start learning from people who are already doing what you want to do.

Don't be afraid to contact experts and talk to them directly. You'll be surprised at how many of them are flattered and more than willing to help someone who shares the same dream. Chances are that if they are successful, someone helped them along once, and they will be happy to pass along the favor. Make a list of ten people who you think might be able to help you, famous or not. Then do some research to see if you can find contact information for any or all of them. Send some emails, stating your name, your dream, your desire to talk to them, and why you chose them. Even if they don't have time to talk to you personally for an informational interview, they might be able to advise you via email or offer to introduce you to others who can help you.

If you can't communicate directly with an expert in your field, do the next best thing and find out how she got to where she is. You can do this by checking out her Wikipedia entry or, better yet, by finding her biography in the library. Just knowing that someone faced the same problems you did, yet found a way to succeed, can help inspire you when you get discouraged.

EFREN: When I was getting interested in acting, I read many books on acting, including biographies of actors I admired, like Johnny Depp and Sean

Penn. I found out some really interesting things about their paths to success and got some comfort from the fact that they struggled for years before they hit it big.

Although experts can teach you specifics about their fields, you can learn valuable skills from everybody around you. For example, if you are a budding actor and your mentor doesn't return your email, you'll need to think about who else can help you succeed and find experts in that field. For a start, you'll need to convince an agent to take you as a client, and you'll need to promote yourself to casting directors. Both of these skills are essentially sales and marketing (for a product called "you"). Find someone who's good at sales and learn how he presents himself and his products to close a sale. Even if that person sells vacuum cleaners, you'll be surprised at how many of his skills you can apply to your own dream.

 DIRECTOR'S NOTES: The more you can learn from others who have reached your dream, the more you'll learn about how to reach that dream.

Get to Know Yourself through Talking with Others

Besides learning about your chosen field from experts and learning about different skill sets from just about anyone, you can also learn a lot about yourself by talking to others. Everyone has strengths and weaknesses. But sometimes we can't see which ones are working for us and which ones are working against us. And sometimes we need others to articulate our dream for us.

Take the example of a young boy who grew up with three other siblings in a family that moved over 20 times by the time he was seven years old. By the time he turned 15, his parents had divorced, and he went through a very difficult time. But he also dreamed of becoming a musician. So he learned to play the guitar and dropped out of high school to join a band. But after just two weeks, he regretted his decision and tried to reenroll in high school. To his surprise, his own high school principal suggested that he stay out of school and try to become a rock star.

This young man soon got married. For money, he held a variety of odd jobs, including working as a telemarketer selling ink pens. His wife introduced him to the actor Nicolas Cage, who saw something in this young man that he'd never seen in himself. Cage suggested that this young man pursue an acting career instead a music career. Today, we all know this young man: Johnny Depp. He might never have achieved the success he craved if not for people like his high school principal and Nicolas Cage, who saw talent in him that he didn't know he had and gave him encouragement to go out and make the most of it.

EFREN: I had a small role in the film *Mr. & Mrs. Smith,* and on the set, I was able to spend time with Angelina Jolie and Brad Pitt. I remember Brad telling me, "Picture where you want to be and go there." The words are easy; the actions are not.

It's usually easy for you to recognize your strengths, but trying to identify your faults can be difficult. Here's another area where other people can help you out by providing an outside perspective. They may notice some less-than-positive traits and characteristics of yours (maybe you're a procrastinator, a flake, a control freak) that are standing in your way—and they may even be able to help you get these traits to work *for* you instead of against you. It's always easier to see the flaws and talents of others than it is to see the flaws and talents in ourselves. Of course, you're not alone. Even star athletes like Tiger Woods and LeBron James still work with coaches so they can get targeted feedback on their performance.

 DIRECTOR'S NOTES: Other people can see traits about you—good and bad—that you may not consciously know about yourself.

Learn How to Work with Others

No matter what your dream may be, even if it's to fly solo around the world in a hot air balloon, you'll always need to work with other people. Here's the good thing about that: they have dreams too, and if you can help them reach their dreams, they'll help you reach yours.

A lot of people forget this. Instead of trying to help others, they wait for others to help them. Instead of looking for opportunities, they wait for opportunities to appear out of the clear blue sky. While waiting for success or for other people to do their work for them, they can spend their whole lives doing nothing but waiting.

For example, if you've ever applied for a job, you've filled out an application and turned in a resume. In other words, you've done exactly what everyone else does when they look for a job. You may have thought that the application process was over, but submitting an application and resume is only the first step toward getting a job, not the last one. Turning in a job application or resume is like buying a lottery ticket. Your chance of success depends mostly on luck. But if you focus on what the company is looking for (i.e., what the other person wants), you will be able to make your resume stand out.

CHRIS: When Luke and I were trying to figure out how to pay for college, we knew we needed a lot of money. How we arrived at the idea to offer ourselves for corporate sponsorship was by thinking about how we could help a corporation get its message out to the world. It was only because we thought of how we could help someone who could help us that our dream came true.

Suppose you're applying for an engineering job at NASA. You know your resume will be one of the many that a human resources director may look at. What can you do to make yours stand out? You can start by doing some research and finding out exactly what the company is looking for. There's a big difference between a design engineer at NASA, a design engineer at General Motors, and a design engineer at IBM. They may all have the same title, but the skills required to get the job done can be drastically different for each company.

The next step is to try to solve the other person's problem. If you know that NASA is looking for engineers to work on the International Space Station, customize your resume to emphasize your interest in related fields and your most applicable skills. By focusing on what the other person wants first, you greatly increase the chances that you'll get what you want, as well.

 DIRECTOR'S NOTES: You can reach your own goal by helping someone else reach theirs.

Find Your Network

Nobody succeeds by herself. All successful people need mentors who believe in and encourage them no matter what. When you're just getting started, identify the people who believe in you; they will often be friends and family. You'll need their support to help you overcome the obstacles and the doubts most people experience at the beginning of their journeys. Trying to reach a goal by yourself can be lonely, but if you have the emotional support of friends and family, you'll find that their faith in you can get you through the rough times.

CHRIS: Over the past few years, I have discovered a great many friends with bright entrepreneurial spirits. Because we are like-minded, I know they will support my new business projects as I move forward in my career.

Sometimes, however, friends and family members criticize your dreams. If this happens to you, you have two choices: one, you can agree with them and forget about your own dreams, or two, you can dismiss the naysayers and go out and find people who believe you can succeed, such as classmates or other people who share your passion for whatever it is you're trying to do. If you want to play music but your parents hate the idea, go down to the local music store and start talking to the folks who sell guitars. They'll be a great source of information on the local music scene, and at the very least, they will understand why you want to pursue music. The more friends you make this way, the bigger your network of support will be. This is a good thing to do regardless of how your friends and family respond to your dreams; the more people on your side, the better.

When you begin networking, get to know other musicians, but also include people in related fields, such as band managers, club owners, venue promoters, and sound technicians. The more people you know, the more likely your network can help you reach your dreams faster than you could alone. Buddying up with the booker at the local venue will pretty much guarantee you a gig—as long as your music is good, of course.

BEHIND THE SCENES: Natasha Komis

Model Natasha Komis talks about how her dream became a reality.

All my life, I have been fascinated with creation and communication. I guess you could say the adventure began the day I was born, because all the childish things I did for fun became steps toward my reality today. At seven years old, I directed holiday family plays that I forced my younger cousins into. These plays consisted of choreographed dances, reenactments, puppet shows, and singing.

In high school, I hosted and produced a local television show and radio show. The day I interviewed Dr. Loretta Long of *Sesame Street,* I thought to myself, "I want this to be my future." That's when I also began to model, booking music videos, commercials, magazine covers, and shows.

Eventually I met the CEO of American Apparel, Dov Charney, and did a photo shoot. American Apparel gave me great worldwide exposure—everything from billboards to storefronts, catalogs, trade shows, television, and radio. It was then that I realized I was on my way to success. ★

To get to know people in your field and related fields, you have to publicize yourself. Attending seminars and conferences, volunteering your services to charitable organizations, writing articles in newsletters or magazines catering to your field, starting a website or blog related to your career, or joining a social networking website where you can connect with like-minded people are just some of the ways you can publicize yourself. The more visible you become, the more people will see you as an expert in your chosen field.

> CHRIS: Everyone and their dog post videos on YouTube, MySpace, and IMEEM, but how many people will actually view your videos if they don't know they exist? If you think you have a video that stands out from the crowd, why not email the link to blogs, news websites, or even your local newspaper editor so that it gets the exposure it deserves? Once a video is linked and people begin to talk about it, your video will stand out from the videos of sleeping dogs.

Creating a network is more than just meeting other people. Creating a network also means helping other people. If you send business or customers to other people, they'll definitely remember who you are (and just might return the favor someday). Interview potential members of your network for newsletters or magazine articles that you're writing, making sure to remind them of the free publicity they'll get.

If you help people, they will want you in their network. Then you won't have to contact others cold when you need help; you can just rely on your network and speed toward your dream as quickly as possible.

DIRECTOR'S NOTES: The more people you know, the more likely your network can help you reach your dreams faster than you could alone.

NETWORKING WITH A PURPOSE

Efren

I am a terrible schmoozer. Many people in Hollywood spend their time networking at parties and attending red carpet events, thinking that this will take them to the world of stardom. Now there's nothing wrong with knowing the movers and shakers of Hollywood. The more producers, directors, and casting directors you get to know, the greater the chances that your relationships might turn into a part in a movie or TV show one day. But where most people make a mistake is that they lose track of their dream.

Networking isn't a shortcut to your dream but a tool to help you reach your dream. Besides focusing on building a business network, you also need to focus on building a network of people dedicated to their professions. To build anything of quality and integrity, you need a strong foundation. You can only do this by working on your craft and skills, not just by attending parties.

Surround yourself with good people whom you can look up to and learn from, even people from outside your field. The more you learn from others, the stronger your foundation for success will be, and that will take you much closer to your dreams than just knowing the "right" people.

SURROUND YOURSELF WITH EXPERTS

Chris

My partnership with KBC Media has allowed me to work with some of the world's most extraordinary people. For instance, I've gotten to work with one of the funniest guys on the planet. His name is Phil Rosenthal and he is the creator of the hit television series *Everybody Loves Raymond*. Phil published a book called *You're Lucky You're Funny*, which takes an in-depth look at how he created his TV show based on real events from his own life. Phil also goes on tour with his hilarious show, *Inside the Writer's Room*, an ensemble act he put together with his *Raymond* cowriters. Being around Phil and getting to go on tour with his book and his show, I learned how some of the best comedic material can come straight out of everyday life. Phil taught me one of the most important things I know about success: in order to be creative, you don't have to pull ideas from thin air; you just have to take a look around you.

I've also gotten to learn a lot about success from one of the world's most accomplished scientists, Dr. David Pensak, an international speaker on innovation and the creator of the first Internet firewall. KBC Media also helped represent Dr. Pensak's book, *Innovation for Underdogs*, in which he teaches people of all walks of life how to make the world a better place with innovation. Dr. Pensak is a really brilliant man, but he also has an incredible sense of humor and a real passion for sharing his knowledge with young people. He taught me a lot about how anyone, as long as he or she is living and breathing, has the capacity to think creatively and become a huge success.

Just because you haven't achieved a huge track record of success in a particular field shouldn't stop you from learning more about it. True experts will always be more than eager to teach young people about their passion so that their work is continued. Even if you don't know exactly what field you want to go into, learning from experts of all kinds is a great way to learn about what makes a successful life in general. I might never be the creator of a hit TV show or one of the world's leading innovative scientists, but that doesn't stop me from learning about the general essence of success.

You don't have to work at a publicity firm to meet talented people. Where there's an Internet, there's a way to find great friends and business partners to motivate you and help you achieve your goals.

As Efren and I were launching Powerhouse Pictures Entertainment and the documentary *After School,* I set out to find a young filmmaker who could help us complete production on the film. By doing a simple search on MySpace, I found Robin Charters, who was listed as a young cinematographer. I sent Robin a message about my project and he showed a real interest in the subject and the style of the film. Then he shocked me when he told me that his father was the cinematographer on one of my favorite TV shows, *24.* Robin had grown up helping his dad on TV sets, so he was extremely knowledgeable about how to shoot footage. When Efren and I met Robin, we were impressed by what a cool guy he was, and we all became friends right away. From then on, Robin was a part of our documentary team; I couldn't believe my luck.

I've seen a lot of movies in my life, so I know what it feels like to be inspired by people on-screen. Many people don't fully realize that the people they learn about in documentaries, or see on TV, or read about in books are actually real people who can be contacted just like anyone else. Since the advent of the Internet, you can get in touch with just about anyone you want. In fact, I met one of my good friends just by seeing him in a movie.

In 2006, I was selected to sit on the jury at the Philadelphia Film Festival. One of the films at the festival was a documentary called *Wordplay;* the film chronicled the lives of professional crossword puzzlers and followed them to the word's biggest crossword puzzle championship. The star of the documentary was Tyler Hinman, a 20-year-old college kid who would beat out all the older crossword competitors. I was so impressed with Tyler's unique ability that I decided I would search for Tyler on Facebook. Lo and behold, he had an account, so I sent him a message and we began to chat back and forth.

It so happened that Efren was DJing in Chicago on New Year's Eve 2007, and since Tyler was living in Chicago, I invited him out to see Efren's DJ gigs, and it was a blast to meet him in person. In early 2007, Tyler was going for his third win in a row at the Crossword Puzzle Championship, and he invited me to come up and see the competition.

Tyler won the competition for the third time, and it was unbelievable to see the same victory I had seen on film just a year before unfold before my eyes.

Directing your life means learning from others. But you can't just expect amazing people to drop out of the sky and teach you what you need to know. You need to be able to ask questions of those you admire to figure out what makes them great. And there has never been a better time to do this, since Internet networking makes meeting people a cinch.

PRODUCTION ASSISTANT'S TASKS

☆ Learn from the experts.
Teachers and other experts can change your life
by sharing their knowledge with you. Find some
classes in your area that will help you on the road
to success.

☆ Be open to other people's perceptions of you.
They may point out positive traits and talents that
could get you going in a whole new direction. They
may also point out your faults and offer suggestions
for making them work for you. Try making a list of
what you consider your strengths and weaknesses
to be. Then run it by a trusted friend or teacher and
see what that person has to say.

☆ Figure out how to get people behind you
by helping them accomplish things.
Can you edit resumes, tune guitars, or draw a logo?
All of these skills can help other people in your field
get to where they want to go, and you'll gain experience and maybe even a new friend.

☆ Network, network, network!
Think about things you can do to get face time
with people in your field. If that's not possible, read
biographies of successful people and start asking
around—people who excel in any field will be able
to help you with your dream.

CHAPTER 7

Schedule Your Time

You're so close to directing your life script that you can almost see it on the silver screen. You've got your script, your budget, and your crew. Now it's time to nail down your schedule.

Success always takes time, although the time needed to succeed doesn't always have to take a lifetime, as we both know from experience. So now that you're on your way, you need to figure out how to spend time working toward your goal. The five keys to doing this are as follows:

1. Start, no matter how old you are.
2. Focus and prioritize your time.
3. Clear clutter from your daily routine.
4. Learn everything you can.
5. Practice, practice, practice.

Start Now

The best time to get started chasing any dream is now. Ideally, the earlier you pick a dream for yourself, the sooner you can reach it and the more successful you will be. Tiger Woods began as a child prodigy, appearing on *The Mike Douglas Show* on national television at the age of two to compete in a friendly putting competition with comedian Bob Hope. By age five, Tiger Woods appeared in *Golf Digest,* and by age eight, he won the Junior World Golf Championship in the youngest age group. By age 19, he became the youngest winner of the U.S. Amateur Championship, and he went on to win nearly every major golf tournament in the world.

> EFREN: Time waits for no one, but we are all given time. Ask yourself how you want to spend it. Is it ever too late? Sometimes it is, and sometimes it isn't. So why wait to find out? Go out there, as the force is within you . . . force yourself.

It's easy to understand how a former child prodigy like Tiger Woods can achieve massive success, but if you're not a child prodigy, it doesn't really matter. You can start later in life and still accomplish your dream.

For example, two childhood friends shared a passion for food but spent most of their childhood doing what everyone else was doing: going to school, having fun, and not really picking a direction for their life at all. After graduating from high school, the two friends decided to put their passion for food into a business. They narrowed down their choices to making bagels or making ice cream. After finding out that ice cream–making equipment cost less than bagel-making equipment, they decided to go into the ice cream–making business.

Not knowing a thing about making ice cream, the two partners took a correspondence course on how to make it from Pennsylvania State University. After completing this basic course, they decided to open an ice cream store in a town that had a college, which is how they wound up in Burlington, Vermont.

At first, business was good during the fall when students flooded the town. Then winter hit, and nobody wanted to buy ice cream in the middle of January. As they watched their retail business dry up, the partners decided to package their ice cream in containers that people could buy, take home, and enjoy at their leisure.

That's how modern-day empire Ben & Jerry's Ice Cream was born. Neither Ben nor Jerry spent the early part of their lives focused on starting an ice cream business. They just both shared a love of food and wanted to find a way to have fun in a business that they truly enjoyed. However, once they picked their dream, they funneled their energy into making it work, and their passion for food separated them from their competitors.

Whether you start early in life like Tiger Woods, after high school like Ben and Jerry, or much later in life like Colonel Sanders, who started his Kentucky Fried Chicken (KFC) restaurants at the age of 65, you can succeed at any age—just as long as you spend your time focused on your goals.

 DIRECTOR'S NOTES: It doesn't matter how old you are, you can start pursuing your dream today.

Prioritize Your Time

Some people complain that life is unfair. That may be so, but life is very fair when it comes to time. No matter who you are, how much money you have, or whom you know, you always have the same amount of time every day as everyone else on the planet. Everyone starts out with 24 hours in a day. How we spend our time determines the direction of our lives.

> CHRIS: I live on the East Coast, but many of my colleagues are on the West Coast. My hours are not the normal 9 to 5; they are more like noon to 8. I never really felt I could get any work done if I got into my office at 9:00 AM. The time difference between coasts means that my emails don't come in until lunchtime; any time spent at my office before then would be boring and unprofitable. So I adapted my schedule to be most productive.

Here are some tips for organizing your time and prioritizing your goals:

- Make a list of specific, small steps you want to take to get started on your dream. For example, if you want to become an actor, your list might look like this:

1. Look for acting classes at local colleges.
2. Go to the library and get biographies of actors I admire.
3. Get head shots taken.
4. Audition for local theater productions.
5. Talk to Mom's friend about her years as a television producer.

- Now break down each step. Here are some items for your to-do list:
  1. Spend an hour looking at local college websites and printing out information on acting classes.
  2. Stop by the library on my way home from work.
  3. Research student photographers who might be able to take head shots for free in exchange for the experience.
  4. Check the local paper for audition listings.
  5. Email Mom's friend to ask if she would be willing to meet with me.

- Here's where you can start to prioritize. Which tasks can you do right away? Do those first and get the ball rolling. Reorder the items, putting "easiest" first:
  1. Email Mom's friend.
  2. Check the paper.
  3. Stop by the library.
  4. Look at college websites.
  5. Find photographers.

Bruce Lee once said, "The successful warrior is the average man, with laserlike focus." No matter how ordinary you may feel, spending your time focused on your dreams will bring you far greater results than sheer talent alone. If you focus your life toward getting what you want, even accomplishing the littlest things can give you a sense of confidence and passion that will seep into the other parts of your life. It won't be long until friends and family notice that you've "changed" (i.e., you are now living your dream life).

 DIRECTOR'S NOTES: The more focused you are on your priorities, the sooner you will make progress toward your dream.

Clear Clutter from Your Life

Just as you may need to clear out a cluttered garage so you can make room to park a new sports car, you need to clear out your cluttered schedule so you can make room for activities that you'll enjoy and that will bring you closer to your dream. The main difference between successful people and unsuccessful ones is the way they spend their time. Successful people know what they want to achieve, develop a plan to reach that goal, and then spend as much time as possible working toward that goal. Unsuccessful people don't know what they want. As a result, they spend their time on unproductive activities that not only won't help them reach their goals but may actually move them farther away from their goals.

Now that you have your "easiest first" list, you'll need to take a good look at how you are currently spending your time. Make another list, this time blocking out your daily activities for a week. Include going to work, attending classes, working out, spending time with loved ones, appointments, obligations, and the like. And don't forget to sleep. While this exercise may seem tedious, the point is to help you see how you spend your time and decide whether your activities are helping you move toward your goals or not.

EFREN: Success isn't about taking massive leaps forward but steering your life in the direction you want to go one tiny step at a time. You're going to make mistakes, and that's okay. Just constantly examine your life and eliminate the things that may sabotage you.

Once you've made this list, the first thing you will notice is that no matter how busy you think you are, you always have a bit of open time. Chances are good, too, that during any day, you'll find that you're spending too much time on certain activities. The first thing you should do is ask yourself how you're currently spending your free time. How can you use that time to pursue your goals? Could you go to the library and do research during your lunch hour if you usually only take ten minutes to eat?

Then you need to identify unproductive activities and eliminate them from your schedule. Replace them with more productive activities. When deciding which activities to eliminate or reduce, use your dream as your criteria. If an activity isn't helping you move closer to your goal, stop doing it or reduce it as much as possible. If becoming a video game engineer isn't your dream, then spending ten hours a week attached to your PlayStation isn't productive. If you find yourself attached to an unproductive activity that you don't want to drop, that's a big clue that your dream isn't as compelling to you as you might have thought. That could be a signal to find a more compelling dream.

Clearing clutter from your daily schedule shouldn't make you feel as though you're missing or sacrificing anything. Instead, it should energize you and get you excited. If you've ever gone out on a date with someone you've really wanted to get to know, you'll see how easy it is to shove aside trivial activities to pursue your date. Likewise, you need to feel that same sense of excitement when clearing your schedule to make time for pursuing your dreams.

Be ruthless. You may find yourself doing certain activities out of sheer habit. Other times, you may find you can rearrange certain activities to free up more time. For example, if you find yourself wasting an hour in rush hour traffic going to work or school, leave earlier. This will cut down on your commuting time so you can devote the extra time to working on your goals.

Given the choice between wasting time, feeling that your life is going nowhere and taking control of your life by doing fun activities that can turn into the greatest adventure you've ever dreamed of, you'll find that clearing out useless activities will be a lot easier than you think. In fact, you might wonder why you didn't do it a lot sooner.

DIRECTOR'S NOTES: Successful people know what they want, develop a plan to reach that goal, and then spend as much time as possible working toward that goal.

Fill Your Time with Your Dream

With your schedule cleared of useless activities and reduced to a minimum of necessary activities, it's time to fill your free time with fun things that will help you succeed. The more time you spend on your goals, the closer you'll get to achieving them. It's literally that simple. Stephen King once said that if you want to learn how to write, you must "read four hours a day and write four hours a day. If you cannot find the time for that, you can't expect to become a good writer." King's approach to writing highlights two important uses for your time: learning your craft and practicing it. You need to spend time doing both, because if you only practice without taking time to learn, you could wind up heading in the wrong direction and wasting your time. Imagine dreaming about winning Wimbledon and spending ten years practicing in your backyard—only to discover that you spent ten years holding the racket incorrectly.

Professionals in all fields constantly take lessons to improve. The most talented athletes still rely on coaches. The highest-paid movie stars still rely on directors to help with their performances. Even after years of success as a pop star, Madonna still took lessons from a voice coach to improve her singing for the musical film *Evita*. No matter how good you are, you can always get better by learning something new every day.

> CHRIS: Just because you haven't achieved success in a particular field doesn't have to stop you from learning more about it—it can actually help feed your passion.

Learning activities include anything that teaches you more about your chosen dream, such as watching an instructional video, reading a book or magazine, taking a class, or talking to other people who are successful in your chosen field. You might even think about enrolling in a certificate program, a continuing education class, or a traditional degree program. If this is out of the question, design your own "syllabus" (with the help of a mentor and/or the Internet) and create your own class in one aspect of your field. For example, if you want to become an actor but don't know how to get started, look for acting class syllabi on the Web. See if you can follow some of the assignments and then pick up the books on the reading list.

Of course, learning by itself is just as useless. Many aspiring actors move to Hollywood and spend all their time attending acting classes but never hustle to find work on their own. Many aspiring novelists take writing classes or read books about writing but never seem to find the time to write anything they can submit to a publisher. It's nice to learn something new, but you still have to put that knowledge to use before it will do you any good. That's why you need to schedule practice into your everyday activities. It's one thing to dream about becoming a pastry chef and opening your own pastry store, but you need to spend every day moving toward that goal. Can Mom or Grandma help you with this? Could you shadow a chef in a local restaurant? Could you enter a program at a culinary institute?

You can gain valuable experience in any field by volunteering or participating in an internship program. Since you've now cleared part of your daily routine, you'll have a few hours a week to gain on-the-job experience. See if any companies in your area need interns, or reach out to local volunteer organizations to see if any programs they run match your dream. You'll not only gain experience, but you'll help someone else in the process.

Spend part of every day learning and doing, and you'll gradually inch toward your dream. Keep in mind the story of the tortoise and the hare. The tortoise won by making slow, steady progress, and you can do the same by making sure that you learn and do something every day that focuses on your dream.

 DIRECTOR'S NOTES: Take time every day to learn about and practice your dream.

HOW I LEARNED TO SCHEDULE MY TIME

Efren

One of the most important skills to master is respecting the time of others. Some people do this naturally, but I learned it the hard way.

I once had a role on a TV show where I played a thief. Not only did my character run things his own way, but he was a know-it-all who was reckless, careless, selfish, and completely self-centered. Little did I realize how much of that character was part of my own personality.

Halfway through the ten-day shoot, I had an early call time for 5:00 AM the next day, which meant I had to be on the set exactly at 5:00 AM, ready to work. That morning I overslept and only woke up at 5:00 AM when the second assistant director called me and asked where I was. I apologized for being late and told them I would be there in 30 minutes.

Every 5 minutes, I would get another phone call asking where I was. Despite these constant phone calls, I still arrived at the set 90 minutes late. The director pulled me aside and told me that being late that day was my "free card." However, he sternly reminded me that everyone else had been on the set at 4:00 AM to prepare for the shoot at 5:00 AM and that I had held up the entire production just by not showing up on time. He was furious at me and could have had me fired.

I felt terrible. Until that moment, I hadn't realized how much my actions could affect others. Although it was a hard lesson to learn, from that moment on, I made sure I was never late to a set, a rehearsal, a meeting, or any other appointment for the rest of my life.

HOW A FOUR-MINUTE VIDEO CAN CHANGE A LIFE

Chris

I grew up in Cherry Hill, New Jersey, and even though that area is a beautiful community, it exists just miles from the small, distressed city of Camden. Likewise, when Efren was growing up in California, he was surrounded by the same kind of poverty and economic disparity. This is why Efren and I have made it a priority to speak at Camden Creative Arts High School numerous times since 2005. I like to think that by speaking to these kids and telling them our stories, we are helping them to change their lives.

Before our first trip to the school, we thought we were only going to be able to speak to the kids for an hour; but we had such a wonderful time with the students that we ended up staying all afternoon to meet every kid in the school. The students wanted to find out everything they could about the films Efren and I were working on, and we learned just as much from the students as they did from us; we were treated to dance and theatrical performances that blew us away.

At the same time, as the 2008 presidential campaigns picked up in mid-2007, I started attending political debates and rallies in my free time and posting my videos of the events on YouTube. During that summer, I got an email from Steve

Grove, the YouTube political editor. He told me that YouTube
was sponsoring an innovative type of debate that would air on
CNN. He asked me if I could shoot a question with someone in
the inner city, and I knew right away that this would be a great
opportunity to work with some of the kids in Camden.

I contacted one of the directors of the school, and she said
she had the perfect student to talk to me. When I showed up
at the school with my camera, Craig Bazan said that he would
like to ask the candidates how they planned to heal inner-city
violence. After we were done shooting the question, Craig
started to tell me a little about himself. He had just graduated
from Camden Creative Arts a month before as a drama major,
and he was planning to head off to college to pursue acting in
the fall. Craig told me that he had to memorize and perform
over a dozen diverse monologues his senior year to be able to
graduate. I told Craig I would love to see him perform, and
he offered to perform one of his favorite monologues from
Hamlet for me right there on the spot.

Craig's performance was incredible. He had memorized
and perfected his diction beautifully, and he delivered his
lines flawlessly and with tremendous emotion. I knew there
was something incredibly special in Craig's talent, so I asked
him if I could film him doing the same monologue right there
on the sidewalk.

I set up my camera, hit record, and let the tape roll for
four minutes while Craig gave an equally impressive performance as before. He didn't have much to work with; Craig
was in casual clothes and sneakers and his backdrop was
nothing more than boarded up, drug-infested houses, but
he was just as wonderful as the talent you'd expect to see

on Broadway. After the first take, I rewound the footage to show Craig what I had captured. He was so pleased to see it all on tape; Craig had been acting his whole life, but he had never seen himself on camera.

I went straight back to my office and edited the footage of the debate question and the monologue. I uploaded both videos, and though Craig's debate question wasn't selected by CNN, I got an email within hours from the YouTube editor, Big Joe Smith. He absolutely loved Craig's *Hamlet* video. Over the next month, the video was featured on the front page of YouTube; it eventually garnered almost half a million views, and it was featured worldwide on ABC's new TV show, *I-Caught.* The local news crews also came out and interviewed Craig. It might seem hard to believe because it happened so quickly, but Craig now has auditions lined up at Julliard and the New Jersey Shakespearean Company.

I am sharing this story as an example of how big things can come from little places. For me, I was able to discover true talent as a result of simply following political events with my camera. But this story is really about Craig Bazan, who by practicing what he loved in the middle of a broken city, was able to step out and shine for everyone to see. I was so moved by Craig that I have gone back numerous times to film more amazing students to highlight their talents for the world.

PRODUCTION ASSISTANT'S TASKS

☆ Make a list of action steps, then order them from "easiest" to "hardest."
If you get some easy ones out of the way before you head to work, you will feel better all day.

☆ Examine your daily schedule.
See what you can cut out and where you can spend time working toward your goal.

☆ Eliminate activities.
If an activity has nothing to do with your dream, cut it.

☆ Learn about and do something related to your goal every day.

ACT III

POST-PRODUCTION:
DEBUT YOUR DREAM

CHAPTER 8

Ready, Set, Shoot!

N ow that you have dedicated yourself to working toward your dream, it's time to get on the set of your life and shoot your movie! You'll probably have some on-set jitters, so let's look at how to deal with fear using your newfound confidence.

Understanding Anxiety and Fear

Anxiety is a natural response when you are faced with a test, whether it's an exam or a public speech. We've both experienced it plenty of times. Anxiety can leave you with sweaty palms and nausea, but it can also leave you with a sense of dread or panic. It can make you want to avoid making a speech in public, looking for a new job, or asking out a person you want to get to know better.

In all of these cases, your fears and anxiety are limiting you. No matter what goal you set for yourself, you'll run into a situation that involves facing some sort of fear, whether it's the fear of talking to others, fear of failing, or fear of changing your life. There are worse things in life than facing your fears—one is waking up one morning with a life filled with "what ifs."

Here are some common fears that can derail anyone's path to their dreams:

- *Fear of failure.* Many people refuse to pursue their dreams because they're afraid that if they try, they might fail.
- *Fear of the unknown.* Rather than take a chance and do something new so they can reach their dreams, some people prefer the safety and security of the status quo.
- *Fear of success.* Some people are more afraid of success than they are of failure. Such fear of success isn't a fear of reaching your dream but of what might happen after you achieve it. Some people fear that having too much money will change their lives in a negative way. Others think that successfully achieving their dream might leave them feeling empty and directionless.

CHRIS: The key is to prevent fear from grabbing hold of you in the first place. Embrace positive thoughts so fear or failure can never enter your mind.

Fear freezes people. And if you're frozen, you can't follow through on your dreams. The longer you keep still, the more likely you'll lose confidence and momentum. Once this happens, you can enter a downward spiral that is very hard to get out of.

We don't want that to happen to you. The most important thing to understand is that it is impossible to eliminate fear or anxiety from your life. Instead, you have to learn to live with it—but refuse to allow it to keep you from your dreams.

 DIRECTOR'S NOTES: It's okay to be frightened, but it's not okay to let your fears stop you in your tracks.

Overcoming Fear

The more you allow fear to control you, the stronger fear gets. Many people run away from their fears, thinking that will solve their problems, but running away only allows the fear to grow bigger and stronger than ever. The best time to identify and overcome your fears is when they're small.

We want you to acknowledge your fears, accept them, and even live with them. The next time you are afraid of doing something, ask yourself, "What's the worst that could happen?" You'll find that most often the worst that could happen is that you'll fail. For example, imagine that you are a young actor preparing for her first performance. Like a lot of other young actors, you are terrified of forgetting your lines on stage. Do you give up, quit the play, and stay in your comfort zone? Or can you find a way around that fear?

If you want to become a successful actor, as in the above example, you have to find a way to get around the common fear of forgetting your lines. Instead of focusing on how ashamed or embarrassed you might feel if the worst-case scenario came true, think of how you might prevent it from happening in the first place. Let your fear fuel you. Focus on the positives and work as hard as you possibly can to make sure you won't forget a line. This might mean studying an extra hour or two each day and rehearsing your part alone after the rest of the cast has gone home. By focusing on the steps you can take to prevent the worst from happening, you'll control your fear and minimize the chances that the worst will occur. The more confident you are about your own preparation, the less fear you'll feel. Voilà! You've changed your role in your own life from that of passive victim to active participant.

> EFREN: I lived my life scared of stepping into the spotlight. But once I faced my fears, a whole world opened up. Now there are endless possibilities.

Now let's address again the most common fears people face when they decide to follow their dreams, this time looking at how you can overcome them.

- *Fear of failure.* Don't fool yourself into thinking that by not trying, you won't fail. Understand that if you do not try, you are guaranteed to fail every time.
- *Fear of the unknown.* The future, even tomorrow, is unknown. If you fear the unknown, what you're really afraid of is your lack of control over the future.

By not taking action, you're already surrendering control over your life, so by not doing anything, you're guaranteed to face the unknown tomorrow. However, if you take action to direct your own life, the fear of the unknown diminishes because you've taken charge of your own life's direction.

- *Fear of success.* To deal with this problem, the secret is to plan ahead. If you think fame might make you arrogant and selfish, write down the type of actions that would make you feel arrogant and selfish. Then write a plan for avoiding these actions. Or if you feel that only greedy people are rich, decide to donate part of any money you earn to a charity. By making concrete plans ahead of time to confront your real fears of success, you can make sure that success won't change you for the worse.

You'll never eliminate fear, but by using fear as motivation, you can take control of any situation and reduce the chances that fear can ever paralyze you. People who are on their way to achieving their dreams have the courage to face and overcome their fears, while those who let their fears overwhelm them never reach their dreams. Which type of person do you want to be?

 DIRECTOR'S NOTES: Acknowledge your fears. Then make concrete plans to avoid the worst-case scenario.

Fear Can Highlight Lessons You Need to Learn

When you're pursuing your dreams, you're going to run into frightening situations, whether they involve making a presentation, calling people on the telephone, or asking people for money. While many people use fear as an excuse to stop pursuing their dreams, you can use fear to help you understand what lesson you need to learn next.

For example, if you want to start your own Internet business, you may be afraid to ask others for advice or help because you're shy. Of course, if you're too shy to ask for help in starting a business, you'll probably let your shyness keep you from getting what you want in all aspects of your life. In this case, your fear is telling you to overcome your shyness so you can progress in your life.

CHRIS: When I was 15, as I waited in line to go up and speak to one of my idols, indie filmmaker Kevin Smith, I was scared. To me, Kevin Smith was someone who had done amazing things with his life; he was my idea of a complete success. For a moment, I felt totally inferior—why would he want to talk to me? But when I finally got a chance to talk to him, I realized that Kevin was just a normal guy; he was really happy to talk about his movie and answer our questions. The greatest thing I got out of that event was the realization that he had dreamed of becoming a filmmaker, and he didn't let fear get in the way of achieving that dream.

Perhaps you want to explore Europe for the summer, but you're afraid of getting lost in different countries where you don't understand the language. Now your fear is teaching you that you need to take steps to overcome this problem, such as learning basic phrases in different languages or teaming up with someone who has wandered around Europe before and can help guide you. In this case, your fear can help you find a solution. So the next time you feel fear, look at it not as an enemy but as a friend that keeps you alert and prepared for the future.

 DIRECTOR'S NOTES: Fear can show you what lesson you need to learn to get closer to your goals.

Developing Confidence

To use fear to your advantage in directing your own life, you need the confidence to work through it. Confidence is the key to persistence, and persistence is the key to success. Whenever you try something new or different, you may feel insecure. But instead of focusing on your insecurity, think of the confidence you'll gain by doing something you've never done before.

To reach for any goal with confidence, you need two things:

1. Knowledge
2. Experience

Knowledge is the easier of the two to obtain. You can easily gain knowledge by taking classes or seminars, reading books and magazines, or just talking to others who know more than you do in a given area.

Experience can also be easy to get, but to get it, you can't be afraid to dive into a new world. Here is the biggest misunderstanding about experience: just because someone has more experience than you do doesn't necessarily mean they have *successful* experience. If you are new to a field, you can gain experience by watching and learning from others. For example, if you want to open your own coffeehouse, visit coffeehouses in your area, and find out what makes one more successful than another. Is it the type of coffee served? The variety? The location of the store? The availability of parking? The prices? The service? Other people have already discovered what works and what doesn't work, so learn from their mistakes and successes. This can put you on the fast track to reaching your own dreams. The more you study others, the more you'll learn, and the more quickly you'll gain experience.

The story of two Americans, George B. Fitch and William Maloney, has inspired us. They had family and business ties to Jamaica, and after witnessing a pushcart derby there, they realized that pushcarts were similar to bobsleds. Figuring that Jamaica had an abundance of excellent sprinters, they tried to recruit the best sprinters for the first Jamaican bobsled team.

Most people in Jamaica had never even seen snow before and didn't know anything about bobsledding. People laughed at the idea and thought it was pointless. Jamaica's best sprinters declined the invitation to learn bobsledding, so the two Americans turned to the Jamaican military. Intrigued at the idea and the challenge, the Jamaican military allowed several soldiers to participate. The team practiced on a flat concrete surface at a nearby Jamaican military base, using a makeshift pushcart designed to approximate the weight and size of a bobsled.

For weeks, the Jamaican bobsled team practiced in the tropical climate. Since they couldn't practice on an actual bobsled track, they focused solely on the running start that is often the most crucial difference between winning and losing in a bobsled race. Get off to a fast start, and you have a chance to win. Get off to a slow start, and even the most experienced bobsled team doesn't have a chance.

After several months of doing nothing more than practicing their running starts, the Jamaican bobsled team competed in the 1988 Winter Olympics. Although everyone thought the team was a joke, they managed to qualify for the event anyway. Unfortunately, during the competition, they crashed. While the wreck ended their hopes for a gold medal, their determination and tenacity earned them grudging respect from the other bobsled teams.

In 1992, the Jamaican bobsled team returned to the Olympics to compete. This time, they placed 14th—ahead of the much more experienced United States, Russian, French, and Italian teams. Finally in 2000, the Jamaican bobsled team won a gold medal at the World Bobsled Championship in Monte Carlo. To compete in a sport that they had initially never heard of and win a gold medal over teams with a long history of bobsledding, the members of the Jamaican bobsled team had to always remain confident. They knew that as long as they practiced and kept improving their skills, they would ultimately overcome any obstacles, no matter how little experience they might have started out with.

Another way to get experience is to immerse yourself in the field that you want to pursue. When Steven Spielberg wanted to become a movie director, he didn't just watch movies. He snuck onto the Universal Studios lot after school every day and hung around working directors, producers, and actors. By immersing himself in the field of filmmaking, Steven Spielberg gained valuable experience.

During the summer, many high school and college students are happy just to get a minimum wage job. However, if you're going to get a summer job, try to get one where you can meet other people who are doing what you want to do. Let's say you want to be a performing artist, yet you are still working at developing the skills it takes to perform on stage. That doesn't mean that you have to abandon the atmosphere of the theater altogether. Look for a job at your favorite theater or playhouse so that you can be around real actors and immerse yourself in the environment that you ultimately want to be a part of.

When you know in your heart that you're doing the best you can to gain knowledge and experience, you'll have the confidence to keep going no matter what happens.

 DIRECTOR'S NOTES: Knowledge and experience
build confidence.

Confidence Breeds Confidence

If you can do one thing well, you can do a second thing well, too. Everyone has done something memorable in his life, whether it's as simple as learning to drive or more complicated, like learning to hang glide or scuba dive. Anytime you're feeling insecure or disheartened, think back to how much you've already accomplished on the way toward your goal and how many things you've learned and achieved outside of your goal. Knowing that you've been able to learn and improve can give you the confidence to believe that you can keep learning and improving.

The first step in developing confidence is to identify the skills you already have. How can you apply them to your new goals? For example, suppose you want to convince investors to fund your movie or business. You may not have done a presentation quite like this before, but you've probably gone to a job interview where you had to convince a recruiter that you had the skills necessary to do the job. In a job interview, you're selling your skills and experience. In a presentation to get funding, you're selling your project's potential and future growth as an investment. The details may differ, but the basic concept of persuasion remains the same. If you're confident about doing a job interview, you can apply the same skills you used to get the job to convince investors to back your new project.

Grab a pen and a piece of paper. List five accomplishments that you're most proud of achieving. Now tape these milestones on your bathroom mirror so that you see them every day. Even if they are small achievements, they're proof that you can achieve something. And if you can achieve little goals, there's no stopping you from achieving a lot of little goals on your way to reaching a bigger goal. Confidence is a self-fulfilling prophecy. The more you've achieved, the more you will achieve.

 DIRECTOR'S NOTES: The more successes you have, the more likely you'll continue having success.

Project Confidence, Not Arrogance

The more confident you are, the more people you'll get on your side, and the more quickly you'll reach your goals. But there's a difference between being confident and being arrogant.

Confident people just let their actions speak for themselves. Nobody in Hollywood questions people like George Lucas or Steven Spielberg, because they have a record of success that nobody can argue with. These men don't project arrogance, but confidence. You can do this, too, even if you are just getting started in a business.

You may not have credentials that match the most successful people in your field, but you do have some. When you confidently present the facts of your experience, you allow others to reach their own conclusions.

Arrogant people let their imaginations run away with them. They don't stick to the facts and seem to have to be talking constantly about how great they are, even making things up to sound more impressive. If you make things up to impress others, you're really trying to make people believe in you based on a lie. People are smarter than you think. Arrogant behavior is transparent—most people can see that you are trying to overcompensate for lack of experience.

On the other hand, if you believe in yourself, you'll attract others who believe in you, too, and that will boost your confidence and chance of success even more.

 DIRECTOR'S NOTES: The more confident you are, the more people you'll get on your side, and the more arrogant you are, the fewer people you'll be able to count on.

 ## UNDERSTANDING CONFIDENCE AND OVERCOMING ANY FEAR
Efren

Sometimes celebrities can get caught up in their own hype and wind up losing sight of who they really are. Fortunately, my acting teacher taught me that confidence is based on knowing what you have, knowing what you don't have, and understanding the difference. You can lie your way to the top, but that's a hollow victory; it ultimately feels empty when you think how much farther you could have gone if you had only stayed true to yourself.

I learned this lesson the hard way. I once took a two-year conservatory program on an acting method called the Meisner technique at the Laura Henry School in Santa Monica. One day, I had to perform a scene with my partner. I had just come back from shooting a film and had missed three weeks of class. I had rehearsed with my partner briefly, making sure I knew the lines, and felt that I would do fine. After all, I had just come back from shooting a film, so I was already a professional actor—right?

Wrong. On stage, my partner, who had spent the past few weeks studying and practicing her lines, poured her heart into her performance, and it showed. Meanwhile, I was so busy thinking about the project that I had just done and how important I was as a professional actor that I forgot about my performance. I didn't listen to my acting partner and only recited my lines. My teacher stopped us before we could finish, singled me out, and asked in an angry voice, "What was that?"

That's when I realized that it doesn't matter what you've done in the past; what matters is how you act and perform in the moment. By forgetting what was important and being selfish, I had neglected my partner, my training, and all that I had worked for to get to where I wanted to be. I remember crying in my car after class because I was afraid my teacher would kick me out of her class, and I felt she had every right to do it.

Luckily for me, she let me stay. From that moment on, I told myself that I would never become a monster with overbearing pride again. I always try to remind myself of what's important by remembering where I've come from, where I stand, and where I am going.

You don't wake up one morning and decide what kind of a person you are going to be. However, you can wake up one morning and decide to do something more. No matter how much or how little you have, you have the ability and the obligation to inspire others.

One time I was shooting a film in Atlanta, and on my day off, I was supposed to fly to Texas to make an appearance in front of thousands of people. Unfortunately, that day I got sick and ran up a temperature of 101.

Upon my arrival, the people who picked me up saw how sick I was and immediately rushed me to a clinic. The doctor wanted to give me a shot, but I told him that I was afraid of needles, so he prescribed medication. Since I was scheduled to appear at a daytime event, I had no time to rest prior to my appearance.

I remember being in the car sweating on the ride to the university, thinking about what I wanted to say. I even had to ask the driver to pull over so I could hurl on the side of the road. Despite my fears of not being able to make it, the thought never crossed my mind to cancel the engagement.

I knew what I had to do, so I drank a can of soda to settle my stomach, washed my face, and followed the coordinator toward the stage. When I took the stage and looked out on a sea of faces, suddenly nothing mattered except for my desire to reach out to as many people as possible to share my insights with them. I was grateful that they supported my work, and I was grateful that the work was there to help inspire them.

After speaking on stage, I was escorted to a table so I could sign autographs for an hour. That hour soon became three hours, because the line was so long and I didn't want to disappoint anyone since they had been standing in line for so long. I was very sick and didn't want to pass out, so after three hours, the coordinator escorted me out so I could go to my hotel and rest. Although I was still sick, I could finally rest knowing that I had overcome and succeeded.

We are all motivated by different things. Find out what motivates and what inspires you, and give back to others. By giving to others, you will surely find your identity and source of strength.

HOW CONFIDENCE DRIVES YOU TO SUCCESS

Chris

To find success in anything, you've got to show confidence. After being interviewed for the documentaries *The Corporation, This Land Is Your Land,* and *Maxed Out* and after gaining experience working with many indie film projects, I knew that I was ready to launch my own film project. I spent a lot of nights looking on the Internet, determined to find an issue I wanted to tackle with a camera. I was so determined to find the perfect topic for my film that I didn't let myself get carried away worrying that I wouldn't be able to make the project work.

Here's why. Filmmaking, like most skills or crafts, is an art. And what excites people about art is being able to see something new. A new filmmaker, an aspiring dancer, a doctor fresh out of medical school—none of these people has a reason to be intimidated by what has come before them, because their films, their performances, or their practices will all be new and unique. Sure I had never directed a documentary before, but as long as I was making a film about an issue that was important to me, an issue no one had ever tackled on camera before, I didn't have anyone's standard to live up to but my own.

So when I first met Owen Lafave, I knew that I had my subject. Owen is the ex-husband of the former Tampa school teacher, Debra Lafave, a woman who was arrested for having an inappropriate relationship with her 14-year-old student. Owen's divorce attorney contacted my media firm, KBC Media, to give him a national outlet to speak out about his experience and prevent the situation from happening to other students. The first interview we set up for Owen was with Cynthia McFadden at ABC's *Primetime Live,* and we couldn't have imagined the impact that Owen's appearance would make.

When he started speaking to Cynthia on camera, Owen immediately touched me with his intensity and his sincerity. He was so passionate about alerting society to the epidemic of teacher-student sex scandals that I knew right away that his story and his mission were what I had been seeking to capture on film. And so right there on the spot, I determined to direct a documentary that would detail Owen's experiences and follow his journey through society, culture, and law to find out why these things happen and how to stop them.

Owen loved the idea. He was really excited about making a film that would call attention to the issue outside of the media he had already been doing. We announced the film, called *After School,* on *Larry King Live* during the 2005 Sundance Film Festival. Our phones started to ring off the hook, and our email boxes were filling up with close to 1,000 emails from victims, experts, and even offenders, all wanting to be interviewed for the film.

Still, for all of this positive encouragement, I had never launched a feature film project of my own. In fact, I had never held a professional camera. So I decided to research cameras and how to use them. But I didn't learn everything about filmmaking from a book. It turns out that the hardest thing about making a movie is not working the camera but getting funding for the project. Getting investors to trust your project enough to put their money into your work is the trickiest part about making a movie. But here's the thing: if you really believe in your mission, you can get others to believe in it, too. Owen and I were so determined to use his story to change lives that getting investors to believe in our goals actually took very little time.

When it comes down to it, you can find the knowledge, money, and talent to help you accomplish your dreams; they're all out there for you to take advantage of. But none of these things will come to you without confidence, and confidence is something you can only give yourself. The way to get confidence is to tell yourself that no one has ever done what you can do in your own very unique way. Keep your eyes open to what's going on around you. Chances are in your favor that something you see will stir you to create a work of art that's all your own.

PRODUCTION ASSISTANT'S TASKS

☆ What scares you the most about making your dream a reality?
Make a list of all of your fears, and then write down steps you can take — or have already taken — that counteract the power of those fears.

☆ Write down the worst-case scenario.
Then make a list of three things you can do to prevent it from happening.

☆ Knowledge and experience breed confidence.
Make sure that you are still focused on learning from other people's experiences.

☆ If you're feeling insecure, list a few of your past accomplishments.
These can be from any area of your life. The sense of pride you feel from looking at this list can be transferred to your new goals.

☆ Tell the truth.
Don't make up things to sound more confident than you really are. This will turn people off, and you'll have a harder time getting where you want to go.

CHAPTER 9

Putting Your Unique
Dream Together

I t's time to take your dream and make it your own. In film, this step is commonly known as postproduction, when the director and other visionaries working on a film come together to edit it and make it ready for release. During this very important step, the unique vision of the filmmaker comes to fruition. This is also an important step for you. How will you make your dream stand out? The key is not to cut out the parts of you that make it unique.

Make Your Differences
Work for You

A lot of aspiring actors in Hollywood have it all wrong. So many of them move to Hollywood and try to dress and act like the hottest star, believing that because Hollywood loves that person, it will also love anyone who looks like that person. What happens to these people? They fail to capture people's attention. No matter what anyone tells you, Hollywood isn't looking for someone just like somebody else, as Efren knows firsthand.

Here's an example. When a young comedian first moved to Hollywood, the first advice he heard from everyone was to get plastic surgery to de-emphasize his most distinctive physical feature—his prominent jutting chin. Casting directors and agents suggested that if he got the surgery, he would be more "marketable." But the comedian refused. And today, Jay Leno, the host of the *Tonight Show* for over a decade and one of the most respected stand-up comedians in show business, has achieved his dreams in part because of his chin—the one thing that Hollywood once considered his greatest drawback.

> EFREN: Take a look at yourself in the mirror. What defines you? Look deep inside, and you will see endless possibilities. Our greatest challenge is to accept who we are and where we are at. Sometimes we think that the key to success is changing our appearance or trying to be someone else. Remember, even if you were cloned, no one could replicate you.

Instead of cookie-cutter stars, Hollywood is looking for someone unique. So is the world at large, as Chris has experienced, which means that you're in luck.

You are unique and special. We're going to show you how to emphasize your uniqueness, because that's the way you're going to succeed at whatever goals you set for yourself. The real stars are the people who allow their true personality to shine.

 DIRECTOR'S NOTES: People don't want clones of people who are already successful. The more unique you are, the more successful you'll be.

Your Differences Can Be Your Greatest Assets

So what's the thing that people notice about you right away? Are you young, old, male, female, tall, or short? Do you talk with an accent? Walk with a limp? Have a big nose, a small mouth, a cheerful face, or a piercing gaze? Perhaps your greatest difference isn't your physical appearance but your personality.

Are you cheerful, sad, pensive, confused, entertaining, or persuasive? Write down what you think makes you stand out in a crowd. Then ask your friends and family members what they think — chances are that they see you differently than you see yourself. Once you've identified your greatest difference, you can turn it into your greatest strength.

You may find that what makes you stand out is the same thing that makes someone else stand out. Maybe you've heard that you look like Christian Bale or sing like Alicia Keys. But even if you share some characteristics with someone who's already successful in your field, remember that there's only one of you, and you'll have to dig deeper to find out what sets you apart from the person you're compared to. Maybe you look like Christian but are younger and interested in working on a sitcom as a comic actor. Or maybe you sound a bit like Alicia but want to pursue a country music career. Anything is possible, and as long as it's authentic, it will be "marketable."

Remember, no matter what you do in life, there will be people with the same dream as you. But that's okay. As long as you focus on turning what makes you unique into your biggest asset, your contribution to the world will be unique, too. Anyone can have the same dream as you, but only you can shape your dream according to your distinct personality, and that can make all the difference in the world.

Sometimes you might feel as though what makes you unique is a disadvantage. But we feel that there are no disadvantages, only advantages waiting for the right circumstances. In fact, when you start focusing on the negative and dwelling on your "disadvantages," you get stuck. But think of the extraordinary contributions of some of the world's most well-known people, like Stevie Wonder, Stephen Hawking, Michael J. Fox, and Andrea Bocelli. To some, they might be considered to be at a disadvantage. But none of them let their disabilities stop them from pursuing their dreams. Some may argue that each of these people used their disabilities to their advantage in that they, through their talent and hard work, are now icons of inspiration for people the world over — those who are blind or suffer from ALS or Parkinson's, as well as people who don't have these afflictions.

In fact, blind people have climbed Mount Everest, people missing limbs have swum across the English Channel, grandmothers have completed triathlons, and teenagers have flown around the world. You're never too young, too old, or too limited in any way to pursue a dream. The biggest obstacle to success is right between your ears. Once you realize that you can achieve your dreams, you've already eliminated the biggest obstacle to success.

Remember, dreams are about pursuing an activity and not just arriving at a destination. It's probably impossible for an average teenage girl to become an NFL quarterback and win a Superbowl, but there's nothing stopping that same girl from playing in a female football league and directing her life to revolve around football.

So if you feel as though the thing that makes you unique is a disadvantage—perhaps you think that you're too shy or too old to start pursuing your dream—start thinking of that characteristic as something that could become your greatest strength. If you're shy and afraid to talk to people, it doesn't have to stop you dead in your tracks. For a start, you can turn this weakness into a strength by focusing on other ways to impress potential employers. Promote your accomplishments on your own website, complete with videos demonstrating your talent and abilities. Burn videos, text, and audio files onto a CD that gives employers a multimedia description of who you are and (more importantly) what skills you can bring to a company to help it reach its own goals. By finding a creative way to compensate for a weakness, you may suddenly find your greatest strength.

 DIRECTOR'S NOTES: Your greatest weakness could actually become your greatest strength.

Don't Worry about What Others Are Doing

A lot of people spend so much time worrying what others are doing that they never get started on their own dreams. Trying to fit in with your peers will only distract you from the life you want. You need to go with your instincts and follow your own time line—just because John Keats wrote all of his poetry by the age of 25 (when he died) doesn't mean you have to write everything you want to write by age 25. You're never too young or too old to do what you want to do.

> CHRIS: There is never really a right age to do anything. When you hear people remark about someone else's achievements, you often hear "Wow he was so young!" or "I can't believe she accomplished that when she was so old!" You rarely hear things like "Good for him—he was exactly the right age to realize his dream!"

If you're starting young, you may not succeed right away. You might even hear that you are "too young" from adults in your field. But keep in mind that because you are young, you have plenty of time to work toward your goals.

Take the example of a young boy from Montana. When he was 11, he took a tour of Walt Disney's animation studios and declared that he would one day work in that studio. Immediately upon returning home, he began work on his own 15-minute animated cartoon. For two years, he labored on that cartoon, and when he finally finished, he submitted it to Walt Disney Studios.

The cartoon impressed Walt Disney Studios so much that Milt Kahl, one of Disney's oldest and most respected animators, agreed to mentor the young boy and teach him everything he knew from his many years of work on such classics as *Pinocchio, Snow White,* and *Sleeping Beauty.*

After graduating from high school, this boy earned a scholarship from Disney Studios to attend the California Institute of the Arts. After graduating from this school, he finally realized his dream and got a chance to work at Disney, where he worked on the animated film *The Fox and the Hound.*

After becoming one of the youngest animators at Disney, he could have stopped dreaming, but he didn't. After working at Disney for a short time, he left to work on other animated projects in Hollywood. He helped turn a simple cartoon into a half-hour program called *The Simpsons,* then later wrote and directed an animated film for Warner Brothers Studios called *The Iron Giant.* He reached another pinnacle of success when he wrote and directed the Pixar animated film *The Incredibles.* This movie was so well received that Pixar asked him to write and direct its next animated feature, *Ratatouille,* which became another box office smash hit. Writer and director Brad Bird achieved success in his dream field of animation, although it all began when he started pursuing his dream at an age that many adults would consider way too young to start anything. Bird didn't care that he was "too young," and look where it got him.

Of course, age can also be held against you if you start working toward your dream when you are older. People might tell you that it's "too late." But let's look at this example to illustrate why that is just not true:

In 1988, at the age of 38, triathlete John Wragg competed in his first Ironman Triathlon, a grueling event that begins with a 2.4-mile ocean swim, continues with a 112-mile bicycle ride, and ends with a 26.2-mile marathon run. Completing any single event would be an achievement in itself, but Wragg not only wanted to complete an Ironman Triathlon, he wanted to complete all five full-distance triathlons offered that year. Even though people said he was crazy, he did just that.

After reaching his goal of completing five triathlons in a single year, Wragg set his sights on another goal: he wanted to be the first person to complete 100 full-distance triathlons in his life. John Wragg plans to complete his 100th full-distance triathlon in 2008 at age 58.

What makes Bird and Wragg unique is that they stood out from the crowd. They proved that 11-year-old animators and 58-year-old triathletes can exist and can be successful. Despite your age or situation, don't be afraid to be different or stand out from the crowd. What makes you stand out may just be the thing that gets you where you want to be in life.

 DIRECTOR'S NOTES: Your time line is the only one that counts.

THAT SOUND YOU HEAR IS THE BEAT OF YOUR OWN DRUMMER

Efren

When I was growing up, my twin brother was more outspoken than me. I admired him because he always spoke his mind and took action. I was quite the opposite. I was quiet, more introverted, and minded my own business. I enjoyed being a twin because in most cases, my twin brother took the initiative by being assertive. Somewhere in the back of my mind was the fear that I would disappoint myself if I stood out. By hiding my differences and trying to blend in with others, I thought I could spare myself the pain and risk of being myself.

In high school, I really didn't fit in. I was a loner, but rather than segregating myself from the rest of the world, I searched for a community. It's human nature to want to belong. I tried the chess club, choir, book club, and assistant-coaching the soccer team. By trying a lot of different things, I found out what I liked and didn't like. Did I fit into all of these communities? No. But I did find some people who could see and accept that I was different.

When I started pursuing acting, I knew that I needed to find my own voice, and I started reading about and partici-pating in acting and other creative arts. I learned something new with every step. Reading about the lives of writers, poets, musicians, actors, and artists, I learned that I really wasn't alone. Once I realized this, I took a chance. I stepped out from my brother's shadow and started pursuing acting with everything I had. I made a leap of faith. And that leap landed me where I am today.

YOUR PAST GIVES CLUES ABOUT HOW TO SUCCEED IN THE FUTURE

Chris

When it comes to figuring out what sets you apart from other people, it's extremely helpful to look to your past. Chances are that the things you loved as a kid are the same things you love now. For instance, the thing that separates me from most people is my interest in and my love for business. I have always been passionate about developing new ways to do business with all walks of life, ever since I was a little kid. When I was in my early teens, I would pick up books just like this one because I wanted to learn everything about running my own company (so that I didn't have to work a summer job at someone else's). I learned at an early age that there is plenty of money to be made, and there are plenty of creative ways to make it.

At age five, I invented labels designed to go inside the soles of children's shoes to help them identify which shoe to put on which foot. The labels were a huge success with kids my age who were frustrated with the left-foot/right-foot shoe conundrum; it even helped kids with orthopedic braces determine which brace was which. I received a patent for my idea a few years after I came up with it, so I am one of the youngest patent holders in history.

The idea to invent the labels came to me one day when I was having difficulty putting my shoes on the right feet (for about the 100th time). I was walking down the stairs, and my mom was trying to stifle a laugh as she said, "Chris, your shoes are on the wrong feet again." I got really frustrated and I asked her why all the adults who insisted I put my shoes on correctly hadn't thought up a good way to help me do it. She was surprised that she hadn't thought of an idea like that before, and she asked me what I thought would do the trick. So I went to my art supplies, dipped my feet in some paint, created my footprints on some pieces of cardboard, and said, "Someone should make labels like that."

Even though I had a great business idea that no one else had thought of, at age five, I wasn't capable of pitching the idea to manufacturers and meeting with them to discuss product specifications. But I did have my family. They helped me move forward with the idea and develop a best-selling product. I got to do press tours for my idea, and I was featured as the world's youngest inventor in *USA Today*, on *The Today Show*, and more.

The lesson here is that just because you are five years old and you need your family to help you doesn't mean you can't start a business. Even if you are 25, 35, or 45, you still need people to help you move forward. I couldn't make a film if I didn't have actors or investors, and I couldn't write this book without the help of people contributing their stories. Recognizing what makes you unique is what sets you off on the right path to your dreams, but realizing what makes others stand out is how you put together a winning team.

No matter your age and no matter your challenges, you can start a business.

By meeting people who have all types of creative careers, I have been really fortunate to find friends and business partners who are living lives of success. And the authors, movie stars, artists, philanthropists, and scientists I have met are all credited with brilliant, unique accomplishments, and none of them is a one-hit wonder or overnight sensation. Success is enduring and everlasting, while an overnight sensation is fleeting and superficial. To be successful, a person shouldn't focus on the glory he might find in a moment but the happiness he can find in a lifetime.

The risk of becoming an overnight sensation rather than a lasting success is something that threatens people in any career. A novelist could very easily produce a worldwide bestseller but then let the prestige get to her head so that the books she writes thereafter don't have the same wit and appeal. An actor might give a stellar breakout performance in a well-produced film but then become so enticed by money that he only takes on shallow roles from then on. But the misfortune of becoming an overnight sensation is most easily demonstrated by looking at people in the music industry, because everyone knows of at least one one-hit wonder.

To gain perspective on what it means to be a true success and not just a momentary sensation, I've tried to gain as much advice as I can from the people I've met in the music world. One of those people is Garrett Dutton of G. Love and Special Sauce, a long-standing and talented music group from Philadelphia. His hits have become classics, but his career has never seen a lull after each of his major successes;

G. Love has been going strong and entertaining his fans with newer and better music for the last ten years.

Many people might think that G. Love's career was born as an overnight sensation, because they first heard of him when some of his songs like "Cold Beverages" and "Baby Got Sauce" became commercial hits on television and movie screens. Even though he transitioned from being a street-hustling musician to an artist with a major record label in just a matter of nine months, Garrett taught me that being a success starts long before you ever become successful.

Garrett started playing his guitar on the streets of Philadelphia when he was 16, years before his work made it out into the world. He had a dream of being a musician and a goal of making enough money to live his life making music instead of working behind a desk. Garrett knew he had a mission to make it big, so he never really saw himself as a street musician. But he recognized that becoming a success meant performing for whoever would listen before he got his big break. He says that performing this way really taught him about how to put on a show, because he was able to communicate with people close-up.

Every night, Garrett used to scout out the good corners to play on before the other street musicians found these lucrative spots. But one night, after years of getting nowhere playing by himself, he decided to join up with another street musician instead of competing with him for the best street corner. The two became friends and started collaborating with each other on their music, until they were producing beats that were better than either had ever come up with on his own. Eventually, G. Love met a drummer for his group the same way, and G. Love and Special Sauce was born; they signed a music deal nine months later.

When G. Love's music first came out, his initial hits were what he calls his novelty tracks, songs that were kind of tongue-in-cheek and funny, cool enough to jump-start his career, and perfect for the movies and commercials they scored. But G. Love says he made his hits successes, not sensations, by never separating himself from what makes his music real. G. Love says that if you let attention and money persuade you to think that you never have to take your work seriously again after reaching a goal, you will certainly find the end of your career.

G. Love says that to keep your career alive and thriving, you have to constantly keep with it. For him, music is like a plant; it needs water and sunlight in the form of practice and creative exploration.

I think the most important thing to take away from G. Love is his message that too many overnight successes become yesterday's sensations because they think money is more valuable than time. G. Love's music has had such a lasting and continued impact, he says, because he puts time into his mind, his body, his business, and most of all his music.

PRODUCTION ASSISTANT'S TASKS

☆ Forget about fitting in with the crowd or
copying other people.
What will make you succeed is what makes you
special.

☆ Write a list of the things that make you
unique.
Then ask your friends and family to weigh in. What
do you hear most often?

☆ "Disadvantages" can be opportunities to
succeed.
Most successful people have overcome obstacles of
one sort or another, and you can, too.

☆ Don't let anyone tell you that you are out of
sync with the crowd.
The more closely that you stick to your own life
script, the more likely your success will come at the
right time for you and for the world, no matter what
your age.

CHAPTER 10

Get Ready to Show
the World Who You Are

At last—it's time to debut your dream. Whether you are opening the doors of a store for the first time or going to your first day at a new job, remember this is just the beginning of the journey toward success. No matter how long you're in business or how many dreams you chase, you will need to work through some common stumbling blocks and stay confident, committed, and open to change. If you can keep that in mind, you're on your way!

Stare Down Stage Fright

The first time most people get on a stage or appear in front of a camera, they often suffer from stage fright. Instead of focusing on what they want to do, they worry about how they look or sound in front of others. This makes them stumble and stutter, which causes them to get more nervous about how they look or sound, and it's just a downward spiral from there.

EFREN: I would go to auditions where I had to dress up as a homeboy or as a Rico Suave-type. I wasn't any of those characters, so I had to ask myself what if I was or who was this character? And I'd take it from there. Once I'd get to the audition, I'd see real homeboys or tall, Latin-lover types. Sometimes I crashed and burned during the audition and looked awful, and sometimes I nailed the role perfectly. I noticed that when I didn't do my best, it was because I was poorly prepared, tired, or drowning in other thoughts that distracted me. And sometimes I was just scared.

The way to overcome stage fright is to stay focused. When actors appear on stage or in front of a camera, they focus on their performances. When you appear on the stage of life, you need to focus on your performance—the activities required to make your dreams come true. When you chase any dream, you're going to run into delays, detours, and obstacles, but the greatest obstacle you must overcome has nothing to do with other people, circumstances, or situations. The biggest obstacle you'll face is yourself. If you take that obstacle, turn it on its head, and push through the fear, you'll be ready to go out into the big, bad world and live your dream.

 DIRECTOR'S NOTES: If you remain focused on the actions you need to take to get you where you want to be, you can overcome any fear you might have.

Be Persistent

The fastest way to success for any goal is constant, persistent action. On the other hand, the fastest way *not* to reach any goal is not to do anything at all. When you know you should do something but don't do it, that's procrastination. A lot of people choose to procrastinate because they are looking for instant gratification at the expense of long-term satisfaction. When people procrastinate, they see the immediate rewards of not doing anything as more appealing than the long-range goal of achieving a dream. Whatever point you're at on your road to success, you need to learn to deal with procrastination.

The first thing you need to do is to recognize when you're procrastinating. It's not hard to do. Are you watching an *American Idol* marathon instead of practicing your piano? Playing Guitar Hero instead of writing a project proposal for your business idea? Cutting short your workout because someone invites you to lunch?

CHRIS: You can still have fun without procrastinating. For instance, I love going to see movies. But although watching a movie is a lot of fun, it's also a great way for a film director to get information. Paying attention to the fine details of a movie's production—the camera angles, the location, the editing style, the lighting—and thinking critically about what you liked and what you would change is a great way to learn how to make films. If you're prone to procrastinating, a good way to have fun and still get your work done is to look for what you can learn from the activities you enjoy.

Second, most people look at the problem as an either/or proposition. For example, suppose your friends invite you to the movies, but you had planned to practice the piano. Either you go to the movies, or you practice the piano and don't go to the movies, right? But what if you want to do both?

This is an opportunity for you to get creative. Look for a third option that gives you the benefits of both options. Here's an idea: share your dream with your friends. Once they understand how important practicing is to you, they might be willing to help you reach your goal while altering their plans so you can join them at the movies as well. Ask your friends to wait until you've practiced and then catch a later show. Perhaps practice just a little bit now, catch a show with your friends, and then go home and practice a little more so you get in all your allotted practice time. Use the short-term reward of going to the movies with your friends as motivation to start practicing right now.

Another type of procrastination doesn't involve your friends at all—it's called avoidance, and you can do it all by yourself. For example, instead of practicing the piano, you decide to clean out the refrigerator. This is known as "doing anything to avoid doing what you know you should be doing." If you find yourself extremely motivated to clean out your crisper, ask yourself why you're avoiding taking action to reach your goal. Are you afraid of success? Afraid of failure and looking foolish? Whatever the reason, you need to

BEHIND THE SCENES: Cameron Fay

Persistence really paid off for filmmaker Cameron Fay, who started out with an interest in electrical engineering but was inspired on two separate occasions to try writing and directing—all because he was open to possibilities even though he thought he had already "figured out" his life. He found out how to start on the filmmaking path, and he didn't stop until he reached his goal.

I started reading my favorite filmmakers' biographies to see what they did and how they made it, and the same school kept popping up: New York University (NYU). The only problem was that I had a penchant for skipping class in high school and, subsequently, not getting good grades, so NYU wasn't exactly realistic. I decided to accept a sports scholarship (tennis) from another school, get the best grades possible, and then try to transfer. I didn't even apply to NYU as an incoming freshman, because I didn't want them to know me until I had something tangible to show them.

So I waited, skipped parties, went to every class, read every book, and finished my freshman year with a 3.9 GPA. When I applied, I sent them some of the short films I had made in the past few years, stuff from freshman year and even high school. I'd call the admissions office nearly every week to see if they'd come to a decision. That sweet lady—I wish I

(continued)

remembered her name — but whoever she was, she'll be ingrained in my memory until the day I die. Her words, simple and powerful: "Cameron, fine, I'll tell you if you stop calling . . . ya got in."

Cut to senior year, NYU. I pooled all my resources together, called in every favor, begged, and pleaded in order to get enough money and equipment to shoot a short film on 35mm. *Fishing for Trauster* was the title. We shot for two weeks in my hometown of Fairfax, Virginia. The crew slept on air mattresses in my mom's house, while the cast stayed in the freshman dorms at George Mason University for $17 bucks a night. With the film in the can, I moved out to Hollywood . . .

It's true, a writer can write anywhere. But what good is that pile of scripts if you don't know anyone to show them to. I figured, why not move to L.A., not knowing anyone, and write while going out to every party, bar, club, and function that would let me walk through the door? I urge everyone to be proactive, make that leap of faith, move out to Los Angeles and pursue it with everything you've got. I took so many random jobs, it'd make your head spin. Old people are the key. I know that sounds crude, but the elderly in Hollywood are extremely friendly. I worked for two men, both over 70: one was an old-time director who'd discovered Robert Redford, and the other was a lyricist who'd worked with some of the biggest acts of the past century. We'd sit there, and they'd tell me some of the most amazing stories you've ever heard. Just a few

(continued)

hours a day, then I'd be on my way, allowing plenty of time to write. I took part-time gigs like this for almost three years. All the while, I wrote seven screenplays. The seventh one, that's the one that hit for me.

I knew four managers well enough that, by this time, they'd read anything I wrote. Four big-timers. So I sent my seventh script, *Unnatural Selection*, to all four of them at the same time. I immediately heard back from two, "Sorry, I'm just not sure this is funny." ("This" being a comedy. Or so I thought.) The third liked it but gave me a slew of notes, a lot of them quite good actually. The final one didn't even read it. I kept begging him to, and he always said he'd get to it "this weekend" but, alas, never did. It was only then that I realized something: managers at different companies rarely speak to each other, especially about unknown, prospective clients. I told the third manager, the one with the notes, that the fourth had read it and loved it! I then told the fourth, the one who hadn't read it at all, that the third had loved it so much, he was ready to sign me. Not to be outdone, the fourth actually read it that weekend. Before he could get back to me, the third called and said he'd read it one last time and realized it wasn't for him. So in the boldest move of my young career, I told the fourth that I was going in to possibly sign with the third, even though he had actually passed. The fourth then promptly wooed, wined, and dined me to the point where I "hesitantly" decided to sign with him. After applying a few notes

(continued)

of his, which were excellent, he started slipping the script around, and within a month, I signed with one of the biggest agencies in the land. Within two weeks of that, I got a call from my new manager and agents notifying me that Universal wanted to buy my script for $500,000. And on top of that, to sweeten the pot, they wanted to attach me to direct. At 25 years old. Less than four years after graduating from NYU. After barely going to high school. After always wanting to be an electrical engineer until I realized what that really meant . . . In that short amount of time (nearly half my life), I had made it to a point that let me breathe and allowed my mom to be proud of the fact that she (probably) wouldn't have to worry about me anymore. ★

motivate yourself by focusing on the rewards and benefits of reaching your goal. Once you've done that, find a way to make the action simple and fun.

Instead of practicing the piano for an hour, perhaps cut back to a half hour or even 15 minutes. This simplifies the task and makes it easier to handle. And any time spent working toward your goal is far better than not doing anything at all. Then try to make it fun. If the activity itself is not necessarily fun (such as lifting weights), at least find a way to make it more enjoyable. Listen to your favorite music while working out. Listen to a comedy show to make you laugh and smile (just don't laugh so much that you lose concentration). Promise to treat yourself to a simple reward after you've completed your action. See a movie or treat yourself to dinner.

EFREN: Look, even magicians have to practice, because if they didn't, their tricks wouldn't be wondrous.

As long as you're taking constant action and consistently moving toward your goal, you'll eventually get there. Sometimes the hardest part is getting started, but once you get started, it's much easier to keep going.

☆ **DIRECTOR'S NOTES:** Any time spent working toward your goal is far better than not doing anything at all.

Remind Yourself Who You Are Today

At this stage in the game, no matter what you're wrestling with, it's time that you remind yourself that you have permission to be who you are and to do exactly what you want with your life.

The way most people define who they are is by their memories of the past. If you played football, baseball, and basketball in school, that can reinforce your belief that you're an athletic person. If you got good grades, took advanced classes, and got high scores on all your tests, that can reinforce your belief that you're intelligent.

EFREN: Remind yourself who you are and remind
yourself where you want to go, but don't label
yourself.

It works the other way around, too. Maybe you were clumsy in sports and always the last one picked for games. That might convince you that you're not good at sports. Perhaps you were shy and never went out on dates. That could reinforce your belief that you're not popular or good at dealing with people. But while the past can influence your current beliefs, the truth is that the past has little to do with what you can accomplish today.

Imagine if you woke up with amnesia and forgot everything that's happened to you. You can't remember who you may have hurt (or who may have hurt you), what embarrassing mistakes you might have made, what traumatic events might have changed your life, or what other people may have said you can or cannot do. Imagine you're essentially the same person you are right now but with no emotional baggage from the past to weigh you down. Given the same skills you have now and the ability to focus 100 percent on pursuing your dreams, don't you think your odds of success might look pretty good?

The reality is that you don't need amnesia to dump the baggage from the past, because the only person keeping the memories of the past alive is you. Don't let the past define who you are today. For example, think of a teenage girl growing up in Los Angeles who was picked on by her classmates. This girl could have let her classmates' insults convince her that she was ugly, but she ignored their taunts and at age 17 moved to Paris and started a modeling career. She grew up to be the famous supermodel and television talk show host Tyra Banks.

Like Tyra, let the past motivate you but not define you. Your reactions to the past define who you are today. Who you decide to be today can influence who you will be tomorrow. If you focus on becoming the type of person who can achieve your dreams today, there's a good chance you'll achieve success as that same type of person in the future. Your future success in life always begins with today.

 DIRECTOR'S NOTES: Your past represents a large part of who you are, but your reactions to the past define who you are today.

Stay Open to Change

You know what you want. But just because you know what you want doesn't mean that you can be closed to the possibility of change. You need to continue to change your lifestyle to maintain your dreams.

Besides making changes in your daily schedule and in your attitude toward advice and criticism, you need to understand that you'll never have everything "figured out" and will never stop working. The harder you work, the more opportunities will come your way. You don't want to be so locked into your dream that you can't see a good opportunity when it presents itself. For example, say your dream is to become a novelist. So you start writing short stories and submitting them to literary journals, and one of your stories is published. What if a television writer happens to read that story and contacts you, asking if you want to collaborate on a television script? Would you say no because your goal is to be a novelist, not a TV writer? Even though it might be uncharted territory for you and even though TV writing was not part of your original plan, this is an opportunity to expand and challenge yourself. And staying committed to staying challenged is a surefire way to become even more successful than you ever dreamed. Even if the script goes nowhere, you will have gained valuable experience—and maybe even a new colleague. Plus, you can still work on your novel.

> CHRIS: When I agreed to be interviewed by a Canadian documentary team about my corporate sponsorship, I never dreamed that I'd end up in a documentary that won the Audience Award at Sundance. Because I remained open, I found a whole new career in filmmaking.

It used to be that people got jobs with a big company, stayed with it for 20 years, and retired with a pension. Those days are long gone. What worked before won't work today, and that's why you need to be open to change just to maintain what you have.

 DIRECTOR'S NOTES: Just because you know what your plan is doesn't mean that you should stop being open to new opportunities for change.

FORGET ABOUT OTHERS, AND CONCENTRATE ON YOURSELF

Efren

One time I had an audition for a TV show where I had to memorize 50 pages of lines. Even worse, the character was a forensic pathologist, which required understanding and using medical terms. I knew I could remember my lines and I could even pretend I knew what I was saying, but to enhance my performance, I did research not only on where the character was from but on what exactly a forensic pathologist did.

For several days, I researched forensic pathology on the Internet and in books. When I got to the studio, I showed up with my head shot, resume, the script pages (called "sides"), my dictionary, my encyclopedias, and my notes. Most of the other actors auditioning for that part looked as if they'd come straight out of a soap opera, and I thought for a moment, "How can I compete against that?"

Then I realized that I wasn't competing against the other actors; I was going into a room to audition in front of a producer and casting director, and the only person they were going to see for that moment was me. It didn't matter what other people looked like, how much more experience they might have, or how many more parts they may have gotten in the past. What mattered was my performance right at that moment.

The producer and casting director were surprised at the research, the diagrams, and the notes that I had made. Buoyed with the confidence of my research, I gave a great performance and owned the room. I didn't get the part, but I still learned a valuable lesson: no matter what your dream may be, you can control your destiny by your commitment to it. The more you commit yourself to achieving your dream, the more you'll feel that you deserve to have your dream.

DREAMS NEVER HAVE TO DIE, BUT THEY MIGHT HAVE TO ADAPT

Chris

The power of radio has been a very strong influence in my life. The media tour for my corporate sponsorship search was launched on the radio. Without the buzz that radio announcement created, the campaign wouldn't have been able to reach a national level and attract the sponsorship with First USA. Radio literally changed my life.

Radio has made my life a lot of fun, too. I grew up in the Philadelphia market, which is one of the top five cities for radio in America. Because of this, I was introduced to all kinds of new music pretty early in my life, and I became a fan of some really great radio personalities and talk show hosts. It was always a real letdown when one of my favorite stations changed its music style or went off the air altogether. The first time this happened, I was 11 years old and was pretty shocked to come home and turn on my favorite top-40 station only to hear smooth jazz!

In time, I came to love another radio station, WDRE. The head of the station was Jim McGuinn, and he did a fantastic job getting the best modern rock music on the air. The station built up a huge fan base, so it was a surprise when the station got sold to Radio One, and the format got flipped over to a hip-hop station called "The Beat." The station let go of its entire rock staff, and Jim ended up working at Philadelphia's Y100, another modern rock station similar to WDRE.

Jim brought his passion to this new station, and over time, he helped create a strong Y100 brand. The station held two major concerts for its fans each year, and it would sponsor smaller events called Sonic Sessions, in which famous bands would perform in a music studio to 50 lucky people. So many people in Philadelphia loved Y100 that when the station got really popular, people driving around the city were bound to spot a Y100 bumper sticker on every third car they saw. Y100 became more than just a radio station; it was a network of artists and fans that made the world of rock music a really personal and special experience to everyone involved. A lot of people in Philadelphia were devastated when Y100 got sold and 103.9's The Beat bounced into Y100's spot on the dial.

Fortunately, Jim and the staff at Y100 were smart; right before Y100 got sold, they noticed the corporate changes and predicted that the flip was coming. Y100 was the last modern or alternative rock station in Philadelphia, and if its music couldn't reach its fans, there would be a gaping hole in the realm of Philadelphia radio. Because they predicted this would happen, the team was able to set up Y100Rocks.com as the station got shut down. Josh Landow, the Web master for Y100, sent out a mass email to the Y100 fan base to let everyone know that Y100 would bring modern rock back to Philadelphia by starting an online radio station. When I found out about the movement to bring the station back online, I knew immediately that I wanted to help the cause.

I contacted Jim McGuinn and let him know I had been a loyal listener of his since I was a teenager and that since I'd become a partner in KBC, I wanted to help get Y100 the press it needed to bring the station back. KBC became an official partner with Y100Rocks, and we brought a lot of local exposure to the story. We even got Y100 a TV spot live from their "bunker" studio in Jim's South Philly house. Over time, Y100 rediscovered all of its fans online; the site got even bigger as listeners became able to tune into the station through their iTunes or through the website itself. Eventually, Y100 online was attracting millions of listeners from around the world.

Y100 became so big online, it proved itself in the music world and made it back to the radio. One day, after Y100 had existed off the radio for over a year, Efren was a guest DJ on the station when it announced it was going back on the air. Jim McGuinn was able to declare that Y100Rocks would become Y-Rock on XPN (*www.yrockonxpn.org*). In the end, being kicked off the radio for a little while turned out to be a good thing: Y100 would still stream to its out-of-Philly fans 24/7 online, but three nights a week, it would get airtime on WXPN, one of the top public radio stations in the country.

Even when something you are passionate about is about to collapse, there is always another way to bring it back or have it start fresh. Just because a company or organization like a radio network wants to shut down the music station you love doesn't mean that that music doesn't deserve to be played or that you don't deserve to hear it. Talent and art will always have a home, even if it has to rent out a space online for a bit.

PRODUCTION ASSISTANT'S TASKS

☆ **Face stage fright head on.**
Focus on the actions you need to take to make your dream a reality.

☆ **Learn to identify and overcome procrastination.**
Delaying your dream does no one any good—least of all you.

☆ **Let go of the past.**
Start seeing yourself as who you are today—someone with a life's purpose, a dream, something to work for.

☆ **Just because you've figured out what you want to do, your work is not done.**
Remain open to possibilities, suggestions, and opportunities that may stretch your dream toward new directions.

Afterword

At this point, you may not know what you want to do with the rest of your life, and that's fine—you have all of the tools you'll need to make it happen when the time comes. But we don't want you to put this book down without at least committing yourself to taking one step toward finding and achieving your dream. We want the lessons you've learned about discovering and realizing your dreams to stick with you and grow stronger from this moment on. Here is the map to follow when directing your own life:

1. *Identify your dream.* A life script starts with an idea—a dream that gives your life direction. Until you find your dream, you won't know how to use your talent and skills. Identifying your dream is the most important step you must take right now.

2. *Edit your life script.* A dream can give you a direction, but is this truly the direction you want to go in, or is it really someone else's dream for you? Make sure you pick the right dream that comes from your heart.

3. *Write your script—and have fun.* Whatever dream you set for yourself, make sure it's rewarding. If it's not fun and it doesn't help others, it's not the right dream. If you can't enjoy the journey, you won't enjoy the result.

4. *Pitch your idea to friends and family—and, most importantly, to yourself.* Give yourself permission to succeed. Once you trust yourself, nothing else can stop you, not even criticism from other people.

5. *Make a concrete plan for success.* Start local, start small . . . just start! Every dream has a price in terms of time and money. If you don't have enough money to get started, you can always get creative and find a way to get started without any money.

6. *Assemble a cast and crew to help you get to where you want to go.* People are always part of any dream. Learn from others' examples, knowledge, opinions, and experiences. Find a network of people who will support your dream.

7. *Schedule your time to focus on your dream.* Get your priorities straight, and reorganize your daily schedule to accommodate your new passion.

8. *Overcome your fears and start your project with confidence.* Fear is natural, but you don't have to let fear stop you from reaching your goals. Develop confidence to help you get past your fears.

9. *Put it all together and get ready for success.* Stay true to yourself—who you are and what you are passionate about are the most important assets you have going for you. It doesn't matter how old you are or where you are in life, you can start pursuing your dreams now.

10. *Show the world your dream.* Cast stage fright and procrastination into the garbage bin. Remind yourself why you are doing what you are doing, and stay open to new possibilities that you've never dreamed of.

While directing your own life should involve all of the above steps, there is no exact order you need to follow. Let the act of directing your own life begin right now with how you choose to make the lessons in this book your own. If you haven't yet found the right project or career move to aspire to, make it a goal now to learn how to network with friends in fields you think you might be interested in. Opportunity can be accessed by the simplest things in life, like watching a documentary or making a new friend. As you move through life searching for the opportunity that's right for you, make sure you seize all other opportunities in the process; the right one may be a diamond in the rough.

Remember, also, that opportunities do not own you, and just because you've achieved success in one area of life doesn't mean you shouldn't branch out and try something new if that's what you feel you should do. Think of yourself as a movie director and the major experiences of your life as your movies. A director like Wes Anderson might have garnered some serious attention for his first movie, *Bottle Rocket,* but he didn't become a legend until he directed a much greater collection of films like *Rushmore, The Royal Tenenbaums,* and *The Darjeeling Limited.*

As the director of your life, you shouldn't just aim to achieve only one goal without planning to step out to achieve something more. Variety is the spice of life, and as a director, you should always be seeking new experiences to build upon your existing success. This is why you should never be scared to choose a major in college, accept a job at a corporation, or try to start a career as an athlete—you are never "stuck" doing one thing. Achieving success doesn't mean climbing a mountain and staying there forever. Success means climbing that mountain and coming down a smarter, wiser, and more insightful person, a person who might want to write a book or direct a movie about that mountain to expand on the achievement.

 DIRECTOR'S NOTES: The longest journey begins by first deciding which way you want to go in the first place.

REACHING YOUR DREAM MAY NOT ALWAYS BE EASY, BUT IT'S ALWAYS WORTH IT

Efren

There was a time when my life was difficult, and I didn't have any idea how to make it better. I was sitting in my car parked on the street late at night. It was so cold that I used my jacket to cover the cracks around the door and had wrapped a blanket tightly around me to stay warm. All I wanted to do was get through the night.

Sometime past midnight, I was awakened by the sound of someone tapping on my window. It was a police officer. He wanted to know what I was doing because I wasn't supposed to park in the spot where I was parked. I had to think of something quickly to tell him, so I told him that I'd gotten into an argument with my girlfriend. He checked my license and registration and told me that it would be best to be on my way.

You see, I had to come up with a lie because I couldn't bring myself to tell him that I was living in my car. I didn't want to tell him because I had too much pride to admit my mistakes to him, or to my parents. They didn't know where I was living because I was afraid to admit that I had failed at trying to live on my own, even though my father had told me, "You are always welcome back home."

One of the greatest enemies that we can face is self-doubt. But what helped me to believe in myself when I was most afraid were the people who cared about me. My life is different now. I am grateful to own a home — I even helped my parents buy a house. I am thankful that I have great people around me. And I am fortunate that I enjoy my job. I enjoy speaking at charity events, universities, high schools, elementary schools, and community organizations. I still have my own struggles and my own battles. I know that I won't get every part out there, and I do get disheartened sometimes, but that's okay. It's a work in progress, and I keep moving forward. And I also know that when I go back home, I still have to wash the dishes, take out the garbage, water my plants, and do my own laundry.

Brad Pitt once told me, "Picture where you want to be and go there." John Travolta told me, "Keep doing it. Never stop." Angelina Jolie told me, "I spent years in the theater before I was able to move forward. We have responsibilities to ourselves and to the world because we can make a difference."

Now I'm challenging you. Pick a dream, pursue it with all your heart, and never give up. You can make a difference, and I look forward to seeing what you can do.

YOU ARE MORE THAN YOUR DREAMS

Chris

I have cowritten this book not as a chronicle of my journey to become a filmmaker but as a portrait of all the different things I have been able to do with my life. I didn't do this so that I could tell people what to do with their lives; I don't want to tell people that they should be artists, producers, or film directors.

And I don't ever want to be just a film director. Of course, right now I am filming a movie, but my project is not just a straightforward film; in addition to entertaining, I hope that *After School* will be a vehicle for social change. For me, making the movie isn't just about learning how to be a better director; it's about learning to be a better person.

I want to be a dreamer and an achiever, and doing this means resisting the temptation to label myself and box myself into just one career. I don't want any of us ever to think of ourselves in terms of just one career, I want us to think of ourselves in terms of our lives, lives that are filled with so many different experiences that we might not know right away what all of them are.

One thing that has helped me experience all that life has to offer is not letting myself feel like I always have to tell people what my next move is. You have to realize opportunities as they come to you and take advantage of them as they inspire you. When directing your own life, you have to realize that what puts you in charge of your life is realizing that you might not be as much in control of your life as you think; at any second, the world can present you with a dream opportunity that you might not have considered before.

Nothing is stopping you from coming up with the ideas, the motivation, and the drive to do anything in this world. You are going to have to work hard, you are going to have to meet people with similar ideas and passions, and you will not be able to do everything by yourself. But the most important thing you can do in directing your own life is to keep your eyes and your ears open.

Sometimes, following even the seemingly smallest opportunities can change your life forever. Uploading videos to YouTube might seem like a step backward for someone who is filming a feature film in HD, but utilizing the opportunity on YouTube to spread my *Hamlet on the Street* video not only changed my life—it changed the life of Craig Bazan, too. And we aren't the only people who discovered a world of opportunities through using a site like this.

A lot of you who love YouTube will probably recognize the name Judson Laipply. His life was changed, too, when he uploaded a video entitled *Evolution of Dance* onto the Net. The short video was shot to document one of Laipply's amazing talents: his ability to perform 30 different dances consecutively to 30 different songs in a row in just six minutes. The video was like nothing most people had ever seen before, and because it was so outstanding, the clip became the number one viewed upload on YouTube, garnering over 80 million views.

Long before he became the famous dancer on YouTube, Judson had been speaking to high schools, universities, and *Fortune* 100 companies about the nature of how life changes. The dance was designed to be a high-energy ending to his speeches with the purpose of getting the crowd excited and demonstrating how even dances have changed drastically over the last 30 years.

As a fellow YouTuber, I started talking to Judson about his video, his work, and his inspiration. A lot of what he had to tell me doesn't just apply to motivational speaking or extreme dancing; his advice is useful to anyone hoping to discover a talent and make the most of it. Judson says that the only way to achieve success with your talents is to share them. He says that sharing your talents is what life is all about. If you try to keep your abilities to yourself to achieve some sort of financial gain, you will never find success, because people won't buy what they can't see. Trying to sell your talent never works by itself. To get to do what you love the most, you've first got to share it.

Judson told me that life is not about being famous; life is about being you, following your dreams, and doing what you love to do. The advice I try to spread to everyone I meet is that if you want to do anything in this world, you have to follow through. You can come up with the best (or worst) ideas in the world, but if you don't even attempt any of them, you will never find success. I've tried to allow my world to be opened up to hundreds of opportunities, and doing this was the only way to move my life forward. Where will I be in 5, 10, or 20 years? That's one question I will never be able to answer, because my life changes with the different choices I make. All I know is that I am going to continue to direct my own life, and now you can, too.

Acknowledgments

I would like to acknowledge my 7 Keys....you know who you are. I would like to thank my acting teachers: Laura Henry, Gloria Gifford, Diane Venora, Lisa Dalton, Alan Feinstein, David Wells, Sally Piper, Stephan Haves, Gary Spats, Diane Harden, and all the other acting teachers who I have failed to mention; my mom and dad; mi familia; and my chemistry teacher Mr. Moreno who believed in me when others did not. I want to thank God, who has been with me every step of the way.

To the reader, I can only hope that as a light you may guide those of future generations and remind them how we are connected and how we need each other to move forward in life. We are a light, and out of the darkness we come . . . –**Efren**

I'd like to thank my mentors and guides; without their support, nothing I've achieved would have been possible. I am extremely grateful to Phil Rosenthal, Dr. David Pensak, Dr. Vinay Rai, Jeff Allen, Steven Beer, and Mark Achbar; I have learned so much from each of you and I feel truly blessed to have experienced your wisdom. I'd like to thank Karen at KBC Media (KBCMedia.com) and Aggrey at Powerhouse Pictures Entertainment (PowerhousePictures.com). I'd especially like to thank my family and Elizabeth; without all of your love, support, and belief in me, this book would not have been possible.

Everyone I have met along my life's path has greatly affected me, influenced me in some wonderful way; for this, I thank all those who have offered me their advice, guidance, and support. I hope the readers of this book will take the lessons I've learned and share it in a positive way with someone else. Life is not a solo endeavor; we all need to support each other's dreams. **–Chris**

Together we would like to thank everyone who brought this book to life. Thank you to our literary agent, Bill Gladstone of Waterside Productions, who helped us find the perfect home for *Direct Your Own Life*. We'd like to thank everyone at Kaplan Publishing for their extra hard work, especially Shannon Berning for her unending belief in our book.

Index

About the Authors

Efren Ramirez had his breakthrough performance as "Pedro" in *Napoleon Dynamite*. He has been acting for over ten years, playing diverse roles in many television shows including *ER, Judging Amy, The District,* and *Boston Public*. Efren's film credits include *Walkout, All You've Got, Crank, Employee of the Month, Crossing the Heart,* and has leading roles in *American Summer* and *Ratko, the Dictator's Son*. When he isn't filming, Efren spends his time spinning CDs and records, appearing as a celebrity DJ in clubs all across the country, and speaking on behalf of charities and foundations. Efren lives in Los Angeles.

Chris Barrett, filmmaker, entrepreneur and inventor, was featured in the award-winning documentary *The Corporation,* has been profiled in *USA Today, New York Times, New York Post, Los Angeles Times, People Magazine,* and other media. He is spotlighted in the books *The Power of Focus for Teens, The Success Principals for Teens,* and *Chicken Soup for the Extraordinary Teen Soul*. He was the first corporately sponsored college student in America, one of the youngest patent holders in the world, and a partner in KBC Media, a media relations firm. He lives in New Jersey.

Efren and Chris speak to hundreds of students each year about how they can direct their own lives. They are also partners in the New York City-based Powerhouse Pictures Entertainment.